The Positive Guide to Divorce

The Positive Guide to
Divorce

A practical and inspiring guide giving you the confidence you need to take control of life

NICOLA DAVIES

BOOKS

Winchester, UK
New York, USA

Copyright © 2003 O Books
46A West Street, Alresford, Hants SO24 9AU, U.K.
Tel: +44 (0) 1962 736880 Fax: +44 (0) 1962 736881
E-mail: office@johnhunt-publishing.com
www.O-books.net

Text: © Nicola Davies 2003

Cover Design: Delancey Creative
Typography: Jim Weaver Design

ISBN 1-903816-58-0

A CIP catalogue record for this book is available from the British
Library.

Printed in the UK by Ashford Colour Press

Restore Information

Restore provides practical advice and guidance to help people
who are going through a life crisis such as divorce, bereavement,
redundancy or retirement. We provide evening events that help you
unravel legal, financial and emotional issues that you have, and help
put you on the right path for building a brighter future.

For more information about Restore, visit their website:
www.restoreprogramme.com

This book is dedicated to every person who has or is going through a relationship break down. I hope this book gives you the courage to not only survive the crisis but also help you look forward to a brighter future.

I would also like to thank Ann Hart for assisting me in the writing of this book. Without her help this book would still have been a pile of ideas and workshop material, so thank you Ann.

Love is absolute, while it lasts.

STENDHAL

Contents

Acknowledgements

I would like to thank Helen Hale, experienced Life Coach and the owner of 'Performance in Process' company, for her advice, guidance and comments in confidence building, self esteem and relationship skills in several sections of this book.

Martin Bourne and Nick Smith from Bradford and Bingley who provided all of the financial information and answered all the frequently asked questions from our clients.

Lee-Ann Farrow and colleagues from Austin Penny and Thorne (Berkhamsted) who assisted in ratifying of the legal section of the book.

Amanda Bristow for her help and support in providing and collating information for this book.

Michael Payne who designed the cover of the book and introduced me to John Hunt Publishing Limited.

John Hunt and all his staff who have assisted in the publishing the book of this book.

My husband for his unconditional love, support and encouragement in producing this book.

I would also like to thank Pastor Willie Gunter and his wife Susan for their prayers and in particular for Psalm 23.

My mother-in-law for listening to me and my mother for being a guinea pig on all of my events and for paying to come on them!

Introduction

I know just how you are feeling. I know because I've been there. And I know it's a place that you wouldn't send your worst enemy, to unless of course they happen to be your ex. So let me tell you why I think I'm qualified to write a book about divorce and be presumptuous enough to call it *The Positive Guide to Divorce*.

Like all good stories it reads a bit like a fairy tale, so if you are sitting comfortably then I'll begin …

Once upon a time there was a princess – that's me by the way. I was pretty, popular, top of the class and always picked to be on the winning team. Naturally, this trend continued into my adulthood – why wouldn't it indeed? I became even more attractive, successful, a real corporate high flyer with a colossal salary, top of the range company car and an all round enviable lifestyle with two gorgeous baby sons who slept through the night in record time – I'm even a natural blonde for heaven's sake.

I certainly didn't mix with people who had baggage, emotional problems, people who came from homes that weren't as perfect as mine – only four bedrooms, no sports car and no account at Dickens & Jones? Pah! What's wrong with you? Catch me associating with losers like that.

And so life in my self-styled 'Magic Kingdom' continued for eight years.

But life and time has a habit of catching up with you, even if you do think you are special and above everything, because one simple question turned my world around and life was never to be the same again.

'Are you happily married?' I was innocently asked one day. 'Yes, very!' I replied, and with a swish of an invisible wand all the magic began to drain out of my life.

I was Cinderella all right – but in reverse. The clock had struck midnight and my life flashed up as the sham it really was. For years I had sealed myself off emotionally, no stark truth was going to penetrate my glamorous façade.

I wasn't happily married; I wasn't even sure if I ever had been. I do remember telling a friend that now I was married I would never feel unhappy again – but I was the girl who lived in a fairy tale, remember? Where was my cutting edge corporate brain during all that time? Perhaps I was under a spell after all?

But that's the danger of break-ups and I dare say you're just finding that out right now. The reasons behind why they are going to happen are seeping into the relationship so insidiously, and over such a period of time, that you may not be aware it's happening – until it's too late.

My marriage broke down because quite honestly I became a victim of my own success. I was working so hard as the breadwinner that I had become merely a bank account and a meal ticket for my ex-husband, or at least that's what it felt like. I had lost the ability to behave like a woman and feel naturally feminine. I realised I longed to be cherished, looked after and treated like a woman.

In no way do I blame my ex-husband. After analysing the marriage and subsequent break-up, I could see that I had allowed the situation to arise; a gradual shift had occurred and it had been allowed to continue without check.

But by the time I was made aware it was too late for us to turn the clock back, the hands had well passed the midnight hour.

Communication had broken down between us; mutual respect and love had long gone and there was no room for manoeuvre from here.

I felt mentally and physically ill. My weight plunged, I was emaciated, I shook, my nerves were shot to pieces and my stomach churned constantly. Once again I went into denial mode – I was so wrapped up in myself that I was convinced no one else could see these changes.

But of course they could. My parents were so worried they made me go to the doctor, who in turn was so concerned he prescribed Prozac. *Prozac? Me?* I was a princess, remember! This just didn't happen to me. I refused to take them. I totally blanked out my feelings, until one day I had to address the situation properly. In my confused state I had driven all the way to Wales, hundreds of miles from my home, when I should have only made a five-minute journey from where I lived to my office.

The terrifying thing was that apart from remembering how loud I played the radio to drown out the sound of the word FAILURE that played over and over in my head, I can't recall the journey at all.

The situation simply couldn't go on; even I, the mistress of delusion, had to tune into reality. So I did the unthinkable – I applied for a divorce. The relief I felt was indescribable. For three hours from leaving the solicitor's office I felt like I was full of glitter. But the euphoria soon turned to the process I now understand as the grieving cycle.

At some point, to try and make sense of it all, I turned to the divorce experts and read lots of books about this pivotal event that was going to change my life for ever. But no one book really covered everything I wanted and needed to know. Some books covered the legal aspects of divorce in great depth, others explained the emotional implications of divorce and some touched on the financial ramifications of getting divorced. Pretty much all of them warned of doom and gloom. Of course I needed to know the practical facts but I also hungered, no, craved to know that I would come through it OK. That there was a reason I was going through all this misery of dismantling my life and that a new life really worth living was waiting to happen.

And once I was through the worst I suddenly thought that I could help others in my situation. So I started the Restore Programme, which provides expert help to men and women going through divorce, bereavement and for those who find themselves in a variety of life crisis situations such as redundancy, single parenting and retirement. It has become my passion and I've sunk everything I own into Restore because I believe that we all need the right support in these situations and should not be afraid to ask for it.

From Restore came the thought that through writing a book I could reach even more people who can't travel to the Restore Programme sessions.

So here it is: *The Positive Guide to Divorce*. I hope you find it enlightening, informative and amusing because in one way, shape or form we've all been there – even if you haven't experienced divorce first hand the chances are you know someone who has.

Via this book may I wish those going through the trauma of divorce all the strength, courage and humour they need to get to the other side – it's worth the journey – trust me. Let me be your guide because there is a path that everyone walks and, believe me, you will tread every sod of the way.

Our way is not soft grass, it's a mountain path with lots of rocks.
But it goes upwards, forward, toward the sun.

RUTH WESTHEIMER

I   The grieving cycle

Whenever I date a guy I think, 'Is this the man I want my children to spend their weekends with?'

RITA RUDNER, COMEDIENNE

So it's all over then? You've smashed the last wedding present dinner plate in the mother of all rows, or maybe you've just checked the credit card bill and realised he couldn't have been at the company conference in Brighton but was cosily tucked up *a deux* in the Parisian Latin quarter. Mon Dieu!

Or possibly you are in danger of committing murder if he keeps you up with his waking-the-dead decibel level, shattering snores.

OK, joking apart, the end is nigh and your name is already in the solicitor's appointment book. At this point let's make it abundantly clear that this book doesn't set out to make divorce the amusing or clever option. It isn't. But unfortunately it may be the only option you've got.

So, first of all, take heart, for one thing's for sure – you are not alone. A staggering one in two marriages end. In addition, take into account the amount of live-in with or without children partnerships that also hit skid row, and we are talking walking emotionally wounded of national disaster scale numbers *every year*.

So, let's look at why people get together in the first place and for three very important reasons: a) that it might help you understand why your own union went west, b) enlightenment is a very fine thing in its own right, and c) it may help alleviate the crippling guilt that accompanies every break-up situation.

Guilt, as you are probably finding out, can seriously hinder your progress forward. Why, oh why, isn't there a government relationship warning on every marriage certificate to that effect?

People tend to get married for the following reasons:

Their partner thinks it's a good idea. One of my friends/clients tells the story of how keen her husband-to-be was to get hitched that he booked the registry office, the reception venue and caterers, and the wedding car, even her bouquet. Just about everything, in fact; well, in the end he did let her choose her wedding dress but he did come on the shopping trip! I kid you not. In later years, when she discovered the art of self-assertion, the marriage floundered ... hardly surprising in the circumstances?

Family pressures – 'You're how old? And still not wed? You watch you don't end up on the shelf young lady.' Usually spoken by a thin-lipped auntie after three too many sherries at a family Christmas gathering, in my experience.

Peer pressure – All your friends are married and you've attended so many bridal showers it's a miracle you haven't caught double pneumonia.

Boomerang appeal – to try and erase the hurt of a previous doomed love affair.

The Jane Austin syndrome – amazing, but true, some people really do get married because it would seem rude not too.

It may perk up a dull relationship – The 'if it ain't broke, don't fix it rule' – but in reverse.

To escape a dull life, job, parental oppression, improve your housing situation – it really is never a good idea to look upon someone else as Mr or Miss Fix-it.

The Narcissus factor – you really fancy yourself in a big white meringue wedding dress and Flash! Bang! Wallop! What a picture! – think about all that attention!

Perhaps you fit neatly into one of the scenarios as described. Or perhaps you got married for an entirely different reason, like getting the UK equivalent of a green card? Or he/she was supremely rich and boasted of a dickey heart but in fact turned out to have the constitution of three oxen lashed together – in which case you had it coming to you. But for those whose heart was originally pinned in the right place by Cupid's arrow, please read on ...

On my programmes we spend some time looking at what is known as the Grieving Cycle. People pass through this chain reaction of feelings at various speeds and degrees. So, first up brace yourself for phase one – the denial and disbelief stage.

Denial

> 'I was in denial for the seven years that my marriage was in any kind of trouble. I told everyone that it was wonderful even though I knew deep down that really wasn't the truth.'

> 'I didn't believe for weeks, even months, they really meant it when they said it was over. I just carried on as usually as if he really hadn't said those chilling words, it had a mind numbing effect on me – literally.'

> 'I tried to be good, didn't argue, I became attentive in the extreme and cooked lots of delicious meals; I made myself into the perfect wife. I thought the more effort I put into our relationship, the more I could erase the fact that we were splitting up.'

> 'I thought it was a sick joke I couldn't believe she said she was leaving me.'

Any of these sound familiar? In all the phases of the grieving cycle just let's drive this important point home – *it's all perfectly normal, you are perfectly normal* – you've had a nasty shock and these are the mechanisms for getting through it. So *don't panic* – you may shoot through the cycle or you may linger in one or several of the stages.

To be in denial mode is in fact very logical because it allows our bodies and minds much needed emotional R&R. It's Nature's way of allowing you to absorb hurtful information and stress at a pace to suit you. So, no beating yourself up about it – is that a deal? You're not being weak and trust me you will at some point move on to one of the next stages of the grieving cycle and it just might be …

Fear

Now this is perfectly understandable. The human condition doesn't take too kindly to the prospect of change, especially if you're the one who has to cope with enforced changes because your partner has baled out.

You feel scared, really scared. What's going to happen? How will you cope on your own? At times you may feel you could turn the clock back even if you're the one who has cut and run. Hell! What if, after creating all that misery, you can't make it on your own?

'I was afraid of who I was. I didn't know how to be single again. What a failure! On my own at my age. The future looked bleak.'

'I was haunted at night by irrational fears – what if I couldn't cope? What if I couldn't provide for my children? We could all end up in a refuge. My thoughts would spiral around in my head making sleep impossible.'

'I was terrified that I would be alone for the rest of my life and never meet anyone who would love me again.'

'I didn't trust myself to make the right decisions so I was scared of what a mess of everything I would make.'

'There were times when I thought to myself, 'was my marriage really all that bad?' Is this the freedom I craved? At times it comes with a big price. Sometimes I wondered if I was a victim of a mid-life crisis.'

But once again trust me on this one. You will learn to cope. It might be slow and sometimes painful; mistakes can and will happen. If your partner was always the one who organised the car insurance or planned the menus for Christmas, or booked the summer holiday and suddenly it's all down to you, then understandably the learning curve is going to be steep. So steep that at times you will gasp for oxygen but when you do successfully complete tasks you've never had to before, there is no finer feeling than the sense of achievement. Besides, who wants to be totally dependent on someone else? Empowerment is truly the positive way forward or, as psychologist Abraham Maslow so aptly stated, 'One can choose to go back toward safety or forward to growth. Growth must be chosen again and again: fear must be overcome again and again.'

So once you start building up your confidence in all matters practical and re-grouping emotionally, whether for yourself or for your children, you may well plunge into the next stage of the grieving cycle.

Anger

Be aware, be very aware, that this emotion, either in red-hot mode or super-charged white heat guise could well strike at any point when the ultimate Dear John scenario finally sinks in.

Remember that taking revenge, though tempting, is never a wise thing to do. And like the old adage states, it really is a dish best served cold …with a thick skin. So please, please, try hard to resist slashing car tyres, sewing prawns into the curtain linings, hiring a hit man or taking that flight to Tahiti for some DIY voodoo curses. Keep your dignity and believe me, get-your-own-back time will come, for sure – what goes around, comes around. So when you are cool, calm and have collected your just deserts in maintenance that opportunity will present itself and you will enjoy that cathartic moment so much more, I promise.

And for those who have done the leaving it is worth noting here, that the pain and suffering you have inflicted represents sheer torture and I'm not using that word lightly. So you must summon up as much tolerance and empathy as you possibly can for your ex, which I know is tricky, especially if you've found the love of your life or discovered your own personal El Dorado of freedom.

But make no mistake, the one who gets left behind is usually the one who holds the cards for the sympathy vote. We all feel sorry for the poor man or lady left alone in the house with half of their possessions, half a life and one half of a relationship. We ask ourselves how she could possibly leave – he would 'do anything for her', they had a golden lifestyle, they had it all and now they have thrown it all away and left him bereft, desperate and very lonely.

When you instigate a divorce it does not suddenly occur one night, it's not as if you wake up one morning and think 'I know, I have nothing to do today, I think I will go and file for divorce!' This decision is never taken lightly, it's an extremely painful, physically, mentally and emotionally draining decision to make and it takes time to come to that conclusion; it takes many attempts to try and rectify the relationship or repair the damage that is being caused in the marriage. But sooner or later the thumb in the damn is no good and just like the flood water pouring in you cannot escape the constant thoughts in your head that this relationship is over and one of you has to make the ultimate, terrifying decision – the decision to end the relationship.

The instigator can be as much a victim as the one left behind. We never ask ourselves how hard it must have been for them to make that decision, knowing that they would, to all intents and purposes, as far as their family and friends are concerned, ruin a perfectly 'happy little family'. The instigator needs support as well, maybe even our praise for being the one in the relationship to say 'enough is enough'.

I don't believe that anyone has to be unhappy; I don't think that anyone has to put up with bad or disrespectful behaviour by their partner. I do believe that it takes two to make a marriage work and so it also takes two to break it. One partner has to make the decision, stand tall and take flack from in-laws and criticism from friends and family. It can take a lot of courage to end a marriage and you are not a failure if you have made the difficult decision to get out of the relationship. The failure would have been to stay in that relationship while it slowly eroded you and your partner away. Maybe we should rethink our verdicts on the one left behind.

As an instigator it doesn't mean spinning your soon-to-be ex a line and therefore fostering false hope or telling them to pull themselves together when you've fielded the umpteenth tearful crack-of-dawn telephone call. If they could pull themselves together they would – they would do virtually *anything* not to feel like their world has imploded on them. But they can't – at least not yet.

So naturally both parties experience anger. The leaver and the left. The leaver just wants the whole ghastly experience over and the guilt to subside. 'Why the hell won't you accept it and let me get on with my new life/mistress/lover/freedom ...?'

The left of course is bewildered with those unanswerable questions like 'How could you do this to me? The children? Our perfect home/ lifestyle? Who is going to fancy/love me at my age ...?'

Quite how you are going to react at this stage is anyone's guess, especially yours. After all, hurt on this scale, whether by betrayal, abandonment or guilt, is mercifully something not many of us experience in life. Men in particular feel so angry at this stage – they are totally bewildered and simply cannot get their heads around why their lives have panned out like this. They often say things like, 'How could she do this to me? I worked so hard to give her everything and now she's run off with a total loser.' Sadly, they cannot comprehend that the so-called 'loser' paid their wife the attention she craved more than the VISA gold card her husband thought she wanted. Others have described their feelings and reactions like this:

> 'I got mad, really, really mad and I hated my ex-partner with a vengeance. All I could think about was what they had done to me; I was consumed

by it. I couldn't think about anything else, my job suffered, relationships with my family and friends. I totally wallowed in my anger.'

'I got angrier and angrier with myself and with my ex for causing me all this unnecessary pain. I used to shake inside and out all of the time. I didn't scream or shout or cry – I seethed inside – and my mind was taken up with nasty, vicious, angry thoughts day and night.'

'I never slept, but I smoked incessantly, shopped like an addict, drank myself into a stupor and laughed like a manic hyena. Total strangers would be treated to a blow-by-blow account of my failed marriage. Anyone would have thought I was married to a complete monster, such was the impression I gave.'

'I hated myself. I was so angry that I could have been so stupid and not have noticed what was happening in front of my nose. Why was I the last to know about the affair? I felt such a fool, surely everyone was laughing at me? I blamed my friends. They could have saved me from this humiliation, surely – even though in my rare rational moments I knew they didn't know any more at the time than I did.'

'I felt such a heel. How could I have inflicted such pain on my wife? But then just how could I have stayed living such a sham of a married life? Who would I have been doing it for? The neighbours? The dinner party circuit? We are only here once; we can't waste our chances of happiness. My anger was directed at those to whom I had to justify my actions.'

'I took my anger out on everyone I came across. In the car I was pure Attila the Hun on wheels – talk about road rage, that didn't come anywhere near it. Life was a battleground. I wanted to thump anyone who wasn't going through the same pain as myself.'

Learn to use your anger in a positive way. It's a great energy provider. Channel all those pent-up feelings into beating rugs, or tackle a job that needs brute strength like giving your house a total Feng Shui style makeover. So get mad, leave getting even for a later date and do get your garage/loft/sitting room straight. And even if you don't feel in the mood for getting some order going in your household, thump hell out of a pillow. Think of the calories you'll be burning and how fabulous you will look when you start dating ... but there's more of that subject to come.

But when all that energy dissipates prepare ye well for the all enveloping feeling of ...

Despair

Crushing and mind numbing, the sense of failure and loneliness can make life seem terribly bleak and add feelings of rejection. No wonder we all seriously consider at this stage whether life is really worth the struggle.

Treat yourself with the finest quality kid gloves when you are going through these troughs. This is just when you should be making sure that you are eating a balanced diet, treating yourself to soothing baths and adding aromatherapy oils, getting adequate rest, cultivating a hobby in which you can lose yourself and so switch off for some respite from the all too painful reality.

'I smoked all the time and cried everywhere.'

'I thought my life was over, I felt like such a failure.'

Don't feel like a failure – you're not. What is failure anyway? Is it really so dreadful to have made a mistake? We're all only human; we can't possibly know the final outcome of all our actions. Only hindsight, as they say, has 20/20 vision.

Is it really a failure to release two people from a relationship where there was unhappiness, where emotional and/or physical needs weren't being met? Where there was physical and/or mental cruelty?

Try to count your blessings, like the roof over your head, bread on the table, supportive friends, a rare sunny day in the grey month of November. Keep positive and remind yourself that this time next year things will be different and *keep moving forward so that hope becomes reality.* Certain factors are absolutely sure. You will discover strengths and talents you never knew you had and you will feel a more rounded individual – ultimately the rewards are greater than the misery you are experiencing.

But for now you will have to take my word for it. And then when you are strong again and really kicking ass allow me to punch the air and gleefully shout, 'I told you so! The drinks are on you!' And talking of the demon drink, please don't use it as a crutch or as blotting paper to mop up all your misery – it won't work. Nor will indulging in crazy bouts of credit card retail therapy, misery-induced banquets of carbohydrates or sleeping around to the extent that you make Casanova look like a love-lorn loser.

If the above do have a magnetism that you are finding difficult to resist, please consult your doctor and ask for help – tranquillizers or therapy. It's brave to ask for help and possibly sheer folly not to. It only has to be a temporary measure and it will help tide you over a difficult period. And once again, repeat after me: 'I am not a failure.'

Hot on the heels of despair is its partner:

Depression

You know that heavy, leaden feeling. Head down, looking at the pavement, seeing only grey or a big black hole that's going to swallow you up and you would rather it did than feel like this any longer. Concentration deserts you; the will to get on with the day and tasks to be done seems futile. Restful sleep is a luxury and afforded only to others.

You simply can't believe life will ever be 'normal' again. You know this isn't the real you but you can't remember how to be yourself anymore. Depression overrides everything.

And no one is immune. The Duchess of York, Sarah Ferguson, has revealed that her life went into a downward spiral of debt and depression. She has admitted to being prescribed medication but declined to take it. 'To this day I don't know how I'm still here,' she is reported as saying. Hello! If she felt like that with crews of servants, bulging closets full of couture clothing and Prince Andrew idolising her – apparently – (you're confused – so was the rest of the nation). OK, I know, she still had Prince Phil to contend with. But it really makes you realise how grim and individual depression can be.

Clients who have attended the Restore evenings have echoed similar sentiments:

> 'I was mortified when the doctor told me I was suffering from depression and prescribed me anti-depressants. I didn't tell a soul – I was so humiliated.'

> 'How could this happen to me? I was always a winner. Everything I did came naturally to me. I was good at my job, a great sportsman, the gregarious life and soul of the party. The depression I felt at the breakdown of my marriage was a nightmare; I thought it would never lift.'

> 'Not only did I feel down, but as a result I was so disorganised and forgetful to the point of being dangerous. I would leave the gas on, or

the car unlocked with the keys in it! Sometimes I couldn't remember where I had left the children, was it Brownies or swimming, chess club or at a friend's? I just couldn't cope with normal everyday tasks. Going to work became impossible, so the debts started to mount. My life was out of control.'

'I was so low the pride in my appearance just bombed. I piled on weight, drank far too much and couldn't be bothered to shave. What a mess, but I couldn't find the energy to do anything about it.'

Most people get depressed at some time or other in their lives but divorce racks up the chances hugely. In fact, on a stress-o-meter only the death of a loved relative has a higher rating and knocks divorce into second position.

Recovery rates differ from person to person and their individual circumstances need to be taken into account. And, I'm afraid to say chaps, but on average it's the ladies who rally quicker and recover from the effects of divorce faster than you.

That's because we tend to have a wider network of friends to unburden ourselves to. Girlie mates worth their Mac lip glosses will listen to their heart-lacerated friend well into the wee small hours, and most certainly way past the hour where their eyes have glazed over with fatigue.

Also, for women with children to care of, the show simply has to go on; well, it might resemble a pantomime performance at times but meals have to be produced and clean laundry must be handed out.

Just as I have stated before, if you need professional help you owe it to yourself, your family and friends to seek it. It will aid and speed up your recovery so that you can go on to lead a happy and fulfilling life. As if all that isn't enough to be going on with, pretty well laced throughout the grieving cycle is good ol' fashioned guilt.

Guilt

No one gets off lightly with this one; well, no one who has a pulse rate and a conscience that is.

As the aggrieved party, you could be feeling very self-righteous and therefore justified in your continuous dips into a deep pool of self-pity. But the chances are, and best get into the brace position now before you read this next bit because this may come as a shock, that you were both to blame for the breakdown of the marriage.

I know you are probably going to hate me for that but often the writing is on the wall in neon, dayglo, three-foot high letters – we just choose to ignore it.

It's so easy to writhe in guilt because you feel you could have prevented the separation, you should have worked harder, been a better lover, mother, father, cook, cleaner, provider. Paranoia sets in, ludicrous thoughts mount and you want to lash yourself for not going to the cinema more often – if only you had been more fun!

By now though, you'll be pleased to read that the next two stages are rather more cheery. As light begins to seep through that long dark tunnel at last you'll find you are getting to grips with the situation and possibly even seeing and understanding why your marriage came to the conclusion it did.

Relief

Many people find feelings of relief and even euphoria flood over them after they have left an unhappy relationship or when the instigator of the misery finally leaves them in peace.

> 'I went out clubbing for the first Saturday in ages just after we split up. My feet felt like they didn't touch the pavement I felt so light in spirit and so happy to be out of that claustrophobic relationship. All the months of anguish – should I or shouldn't I? Would I or wouldn't I? – made it all worthwhile.'

> 'I was so relieved that I didn't have to worry about him coming home and starting another fight, I finally realised I'd never have to go through that again.'

> 'The feeling of relief was overpowering; I felt so liberated.'

> 'No more pretending! Have you got any idea how stressful that is? Peace at last.'

There's no doubt about it that this stage, though it may be a long time coming, is well worth the wait. But just a word of warning is appropriate here too. The high you may feel may come with a bit of a price, in that when you come back down to earth the sheer weight of responsibility may feel heavy. So keep reminding yourself and reliving that lovely lightness of feeling that you first felt on realising the worst of it was over.

One of my Restore clients phrased this stage so aptly, 'I was so relieved that it was finally all over and that I could move on with my life at long last.'

And so we reach the final and last stage of the grieving cycle and although you may feel at times that you take as many steps back as you take forward, with a positive attitude you will reach the healthy and peaceful state of acceptance.

Acceptance

Now this doesn't mean that you passively accept that your ex-partner has treated you badly and so you just shrug your shoulders nonchalantly and say, 'hey s*** happens. Peace and love to all infidels.' Hardly. That's a bit of a tall order. No, acceptance doesn't necessarily mean 'forgive and forget' but it does mean coming to terms with the fact that your situation has changed, life as you knew it before has definitely changed and your life will never be the same again.

Acceptance means that you take all this on board and don't break out into cold sweats. Or lie awake night after night with the zeal of someone trying to break the world record for insomnia or break into sobs when what used to be 'your song' is played on the sound system in the middle of a department store.

Accepting means moving on, rebuilding your life, establishing achievable goals, rekindling friendships and discovering that the grey in your life is giving way to colour.

> 'When I finally acknowledged that she was not coming back to me and that I was not going to die living on my own or suddenly lose my job and my friends weren't going to desert me, things began to be more bearable.'

> 'I realised that I had finally accepted our relationship was over when I no longer refreshed my email every five minutes checking for messages from him!'

> 'It came home to me one day that no matter what I did, said or offered was going to change the way it was – he simply wasn't coming back. I simply stopped trying and using up vast amounts of emotional energy.

The peace I felt was indescribable.'

'I suddenly thought to myself, 'What am I waiting for?' I want my life back, I want to enjoy myself and stop whingeing about my ex all the time.'

Moving on

And finally, as all news reports end, have I got good news for you. After what could be months, or possibly longer if you take to change badly, the moving on stage gradually arrives in your life.

In order to take full advantage of this stage it is important to consider two factors. Don't fall into the trap, now you are over the worst, of thinking that returning to your former spouse may not be such a bad idea after all. You may question why indeed you split up in the first place. Were they really all that irritating and unreasonable? Did they really have such a bad drink problem? OK, so they had an affair but it's all over now and he does seem sorry about it. In fact you're getting on with life so well you're beginning to feel sorry for him. Perhaps you could do a Liz Taylor/Richard Burton? But, whoa up there, before you reach for your mobile phone and make that fateful call consider the facts.

Research has shown that within a year of returning to a previously failed relationship 73% of women and 60% of men wonder if they have made a mistake. It really is better to get on with constructing a new life. Do keep an open mind by all means that your relationship could be rekindled but you owe it to yourself to at least flex those solo muscles and test just how strong you really are.

When you find yourself in a period of doubt, try making a list of all the advantages of going solo against how life was pre break-up and see how favourably it compares.

I cannot emphasize enough how important it is to step up the programme of boosting your self-worth and your self-esteem. And I know I've said it once but it's worth repeating – don't be tempted to take the quick gratification, instant fix options usually found in drink, drugs, over-spending, gambling and easy sex. It's like eating a doughnut when you know you need a decent meal of meat and two veg – yummy at the time but leaves you totally unsatisfied long term.

When I look back at the time of my marriage break-up and the period of time it took for my divorce to legally wind up I remember lying on my bed and thinking, 'When is the pain ever going to end?' It was like look-ing into infinity. But I finally got to the stage I've just described and it's just a great time and oddly enough an experience I would never swap.

So, no regrets OK? Take control. Start as you mean to go on, make a commitment to yourself that you are moving on, vocalise it and visualise it. Don't dig over old bones, I know I sound harsh but your relation-ship is dead so don't let it haunt you by dipping into the past. You have made a decision to move on and remember these wise words: we make decisions but it's our decisions that make us.

2   *What happens legally?*

A woman must have money and a room of her own.

VIRGINIA WOOLF

In this chapter we will look at the legal processes that swings into play once you apply for a divorce.

The legal issues can be baffling. All that legalese jargon for instance – what does it all mean? Honestly, by the time my divorce finally went through I'd learnt so much about the legal system in matrimonial cases I could have played a convincing part in *Ally McBeal*. Then there are those dizzyingly high fees with everything accounted for, like letters and telephone calls. I read a great quote about going to see the solicitor in that you pay for every tear. Quite so. That wise saying 'time is money and money is time' is never more true than at a solicitor's specialising in divorce cases. So do make sure you keep everything to the point and keep the facts as salient as possible. The 'he said, she said, I said's' can be kept to girlie nights in with a shared bottle of wine or discussed manfully propped up on the bar with the lads.

My overriding fear when it was my turn was, what will happen to my children? Was there any chance at all, for any reason, that I could lose them?

So I found myself a solicitor in order to be fully informed and not so scarily ignorant of the facts and in order to set the whole divorce thing off. Choosing a solicitor, I found, is just like shopping around for any other goods or services. And even then you may have to try one or two before you find one that will best suit your needs.

The first one I consulted, for instance, advised me that I should push my divorce through quickly because as I was the main breadwinner my ex-husband might try to claim maintenance from me to keep him in the standard of living he was used to! Which I do admit I thought was a bit rich considering that I would be the one to have the children living with me.

However, my ex-husband didn't pursue me for maintenance and to my knowledge never had any intention of doing so. But it just goes to show you how all sorts of matters can be suggested and, because you're already feeling vulnerable and possibly intimidated by the complex legal issues, you can really worry big style over them and then find all your anxiety was needless.

I was also told that my divorce was simple and straightforward and would take no more than six months to push through. Hmmm, I don't know which planet that solicitor had his office on but clearly not the one we all inhabit because he then lost all my paperwork.

I was then really fortunate in that I got another solicitor, a woman, and she was absolutely brilliant. She talked me through all the procedures, found the paperwork and did her best to make sense of it all and completed the divorce. Admittedly, it did cost me twice as much as I had initially been told but it was over in eleven months.

Now I know how baffling the legalities of the divorce processes can be, I have built into the Restore courses an understanding of what you have to go through when you apply for a divorce. And although I bought all the books that I could at the time, I can honestly say I found them hard going and not exactly bedtime reading.

For instance, I had never heard of mediation at that time and although, in theory I think it's a good idea, I didn't opt for it at the time. However, as some of my Restore clients do, this section also covers the role mediation can have in divorce cases.

So just in case you are struggling too, getting your head around payments, pleads, petitions and the like, I've written this chapter in conjunction with the legal firm that I use on the Restore courses to help explain in the easiest language possible just what is likely to happen, and when.

Introduction to the legal process

At an early stage in your divorce/separation process, you should consider obtaining legal advice about your best course of action.

While a do-it-yourself divorce is relatively easy if you agree that there is to be a divorce, and on what basis, you will almost certainly need a solicitor's help if there is little or no common ground between you. Wherever financial arrangements and division of property are at issue, or where there is uncertainty about the children, an initial advisory meeting with a solicitor specialising in divorce problems has much to recommend it, if only to avoid giving up rights in ignorance of the law.

If you can sort out your financial affairs as equal partners, between yourselves or with the help of a mediator, so much the better – although even then it is wise for both parties to ask a solicitor whether the arrangements seem fair, and to ensure that they are framed in a watertight manner.

If you are intending to use mediation as the primary means of sorting out your arrangements comprehensively, ask your solicitor about his/her attitude towards mediation. Some solicitors are also trained mediators and are likely to have a more constructive approach towards agreements worked out through mediation, as long as they do not work against your (and the family's) best interests.

If it is not possible for the two of you to achieve a fair agreement on your own or via a mediator, a solicitor can negotiate on your behalf. It is not usually possible for you and your spouse to instruct the same solicitor, owing to potential conflicts of interest.

Grounds for divorce

You need to show that you have been married for more than 12 months and that the marriage has broken down. To show that the marriage has broken down you need to show one of the following:

Your partner has committed adultery
You do not need to know the identity of the person your partner has slept with and you do not need to name them on the Divorce Petition. However, if your partner denies the adultery then you may have to prove it. This can be very difficult and for this reason divorce petitions based on this ground do not always succeed.

Your partner has behaved unreasonably
You will need to give examples in the divorce petition about your partner's behaviour and about how this has upset you and made it difficult for you to continue to live with them.

You can use adultery as an example of unreasonable behaviour without the need to prove the adultery. This may be better than relying on adultery as the sole ground.

If your partner does not agree with the allegations he/she may want to defend the divorce and put in their own Divorce Petition. You can settle this either by deciding between you which allegations to put in and what to leave out or if your partner puts in his/her own petition you can agree to a divorce based on both petitions. This is known as 'Cross Decrees' but is, however, rather unusual.

You and your partner have been separated for at least two years before you started divorce proceedings

Your partner must, however, agree to a divorce. If they do not agree you cannot use this ground. You will need to put the date of the separation on the Divorce Petition and briefly state the reason for the separation, such as incompatibility. If you do not know the exact date of the separation an approximate date will do, as long as it can clearly be shown that two years have elapsed.

You and your partner have been separated for at least five years before you started divorce proceedings

You do not need your partner's consent for this ground. This ground is therefore useful if you know your partner is going to be difficult about the divorce or if your partner has disappeared and you do not know where he/she is. If at all possible, the respondent should be located and the papers served upon him/her. The Court will expect quite extensive attempts to have been made to locate the person in question. Again, you will need to give details of the date of the separation and brief reasons for why you separated.

Your partner has deserted you for at least two years before you started the divorce

Again you will have to supply a date on the petition. You will need to show when your partner left you and that you have not had any contact since.

What is Judicial Separation?

You will still need to show one of the above grounds, but there is no need to show that you have been married for 12 months or more.

Therefore, if you cannot obtain a divorce because you have not been married for 12 months or more, you may wish to consider applying for a Judicial Separation, as this will also allow you to apply for a Court Order to settle any dispute you and your partner have about the children or about money and property.

A Judicial Separation means you will remain married, but you do not have to live together. You will need a Judicial Separation Petition. You can use a Divorce Petition and amend it by deleting any reference to the marriage having 'broken down' or that you are seeking a decree to dissolve the marriage.

You will also need to complete a Statement of Arrangements Form, providing the same kind of information you would need to provide for a divorce.

You will also have to submit an original or certified copy of your Marriage Certificate. In addition, you may also have to pay a court fee or complete a Fees Exemption Form.

An alternative to Judicial Separation is to have a Deed of Separation drawn up, which records any agreement reached in respect of finances, etc. This is most commonly used where the parties intend to divorce in two years' time (or as the basis for separation) but feel that they need an agreement in writing in the meantime. To be fully binding both parties should obtain legal advice on the contents. The jurisdiction of the Court cannot, however, be ousted and so there is always the *possibility* of an Order in different terms at the time of the divorce, though in the vast majority of cases a Court Order at that stage would simply follow the terms of the Deed of Separation.

Issues involving children

Disputes involving children are invariably difficult and stressful for all parties concerned. Disagreements can include:

- Where the children should live (residence)
- The frequency with which they should see or stay with the other parent (contact)
- Which school the children should attend
- Which surname the children should take
- What happens if the parent with residence wants to move abroad?

A solicitor can help guide you through these disputes to an amicable resolution. If appropriate they may refer you to a family mediation service to help you resolve these disputes as quickly as possible. Often it is very useful to get in touch with these and similar organisations for advice on how best to help children cope with separation and divorce. Here are some brief guidelines on how to best help your children cope.

Residence

In disputes over where a child will live, the Court will generally favour a solution offering permanence and stability, often assuming the following:

- The working parent who has to arrange childcare will not be preferred over the 'stay at home' parent.
- The continuation of existing arrangements where these are shown to have benefited the children.
- A parent better able to provide workable contact between the child and the other parent will be at an advantage in a dispute.
- The Court will take into account the wishes of the child, dependent upon the age and maturity of the child.
- Adequate mothering, especially for a small child.
- Avoid separating siblings.
- Shared Residence is not a solution that the Court will usually order if one or other parent is opposed to it.

Having heard both arguments the Court will consider the problem(s) from the perspective of what the Court considers to be in the child's best interests. In reaching that conclusion it will normally be assisted by a report from a Child and Family Reporter (CFR) – who will visit the children at the homes of both parents, have separate meetings with both parents, and make enquiries of schools, the local social services or other agencies as appropriate.

The CFR is independent of both parents. The CFR's task is to provide a report to the Court to assist the Court in reaching the best outcome for the children. It is quire rare for a Judge not to endorse the CFR's recommendations.

Where it deems it appropriate the Court will then make an order relating to where the child or children will live. When necessary the Court also has the power to prohibit the removal of a child or children from one person's care and/or their removal from England and Wales.

Contact

This is the right of the Child to see its non-resident parent (and sometimes grandparents).

It is far more common for disagreement to arise over contact than over questions of residence. Where the degree of contact is disputed the first duty of the Court is to make the order that the welfare of the child dictates. The Court will not make any order unless it is satisfied that this would be better for the child than not making an order. This is known as the 'no order' principle and it means in practice that the Court will not attempt to fix something, which it doesn't believe is broken.

The Court believes that it is the right of the child to have a relationship with both parents, and its role is to help finalise arrangements that further this aim. Contact is not a matter of reward or punishment for one or other parent.

What is mediation?

As of July 2000, before you can apply for Public Funding/Community Legal Services Funding to be represented by a solicitor in family proceedings, you will first need to attend a meeting with a trained mediator to assess whether mediation could resolve the differences between your and your partner.
You will be entitled to Public Funding to pay the costs of mediation, if you come within the eligibility limits, and for your solicitor to advise you about mediation. There are some circumstances in which you will not be expected to try mediation before Public Funding is granted to allow your solicitor to represent you in family proceedings. For example:

- If your partner has been violent towards you or you are afraid he/she is likely to become violent.
- If your partner lived more than 1½ hours away from a mediation service, or if there is no mediator available in your area, or the mediator cannot deal with your particular problem.
- If you suffer from a disability, or any other restriction on your ability to travel to see a mediator or for them to assist you.

Your solicitor must seek an exemption from the Legal Services Commission.

At present there is no requirement on a person who is not eligible for Public Funding to attend mediation, i.e. if you pay privately for your solicitor's services.

(Source: Austin Penny & Thorne Solicitors, Berkhamstead.)

Mediation in children issues

Mediation is a process employed when an impartial mediator assists those involved in family breakdown to communicate with each other and reach their own decisions regarding issues between them.

The process involves a trained mediator or mediators, who assist you to define and (hopefully) reach agreed and informed decisions on the issues that are causing difficulty. Mediators are independent and neutral. They have no power to impose a solution. They facilitate discussion and the provision of information in a structured environment.

The process

Mediation seeks to achieve compromise. The process is flexible in order to allow for different circumstances. The following, however, is an indication of what you can expect.

Mediation sessions will generally involve you meeting with your former partner and one, sometimes two, mediator(s), who will:

- Involve you both in explaining how you each see the problem.
- Help you to develop a definition of the problem that you both wish to resolve. There may be questions about who should stay in the home; how capital issues should be dealt with; what maintenance should be paid; as well as child-based issues focusing on how any children can spend time with each of you so as to maintain the relationship that they need with you both.
- Once the problem has been defined, the mediators will help you to express how these particular aspects will affect you. From there you will consider the options for dealing with that problem.
- Often the problem will not have an easy solution and the mediators will help you to make offers and counter offers, negotiating your way to a solution that makes the best of a difficult situation. Ideally this will respect the needs of each to the highest possible degree and will reflect the needs of any children as a priority.

At the end of the mediation, you can ask the mediators to prepare a memorandum of the understanding you have reached and this statement is presented to your respective solicitors, to advise you on the legal aspects and, where necessary, to put into effect your proposals.

There are a growing number of mediation organisations. For details see the Contacts section on page 113.

Modifying your Will

While you were married, if you had a Will, a large part of your property (your 'estate') would have gone to your spouse in the event of your death. However, when your marriage breaks down, your attitude may change. It is therefore important that you consider who will inherit your property at an early stage, perhaps even before the Decree Absolute.

What if I don't have a Will?
If you die without making a will, you are said to have died 'intestate'. A series of rules are then applied to determine who should inherit your estate.

If you die intestate *before* decree absolute of divorce is granted, all of your personal belongings such as jewellery, clothes and pictures, will, as a general rule, pass to your spouse, together with the lion's share of your remaining property such as money, land, etc. (exactly how much will depend on how much you leave and how many other surviving close relatives you have).

If you die intestate *after* the divorce is finalised, your former spouse will have no automatic right to any of your estate. Your children would probably inherit the estate. However, provided he/she has not remarried, he/she can make a special application to the court for a share of your estate on the basis that you should have provided for his/her maintenance after your death. If the Court thinks it would have been reasonable for you to make such provision, it can order provision to be made for your former spouse out of your estate.

What if I have an existing Will?
If you die after Decree Absolute of divorce has been granted but leaving a Will made before you were divorced, unless you have made it clear in your Will that you intend your former spouse's position under it to be

unaffected by the divorce, any gift you have made to him/her therein will automatically become ineffective, as will any appointment of him/her as your executor.

On the other hand, if you die before Decree Absolute (even if Decree Nisi has been granted), your spouse will still be able to benefit from any gift to them in your Will. It is therefore advisable to make a fresh Will catering for your new circumstances to ensure that your property will pass to whoever you wish to inherit it. However, whatever you do, you cannot rule out entirely the possibility that your spouse may make an application for provision out of your estate for his/her maintenance just as he/she could have done, had you died intestate.

(Source: Austin Penny & Thorne Solicitors, Berkhamstead)

Child Maintenance

Since the Child Support Act 1991 came into force in April 1993, different rules apply to claims for Child Support. Changes were made to the way in which Child Maintenance is calculated in 2003 so we suggest that you seek up to date information from the CSA first, as they could change again.

A parent who needs financial help from an ex-partner to look after children may be required to use the Child Support Agency (CSA) to claim the child support from him/her. If the parent who looks after the children already receives or will claim income-based Jobseeker's Allowance, Income Support, Family Credit or Disability Working Allowance, then she (or, more rarely, he) will be referred to the CSA by the Department of Social Security (DSS) and asked to make a claim for child maintenance. If none of these benefits is claimed, the parent looking after the children can still use the CSA but will not be forced to do so – voluntary agreements can be made as an alternative.

3　Finances

Money is like muck, not good except to be spread.

*A*h, money – that clinking, clanking sound that makes the world go round, as the song goes. I must say, when I hear that one they are definitely playing my kind of tune. I've always earned my own money, well, ever since I was 19 years of age, that is.

Soon after leaving home I quickly scrambled onto the property ladder and became the proud owner of my first flat. So you could say I know how to manage my finances rather well. I was a veritable Chancellor of the Household Exchequer. Every day was budget day in my home.

I'd never been in debt, planned my finances with the Old Lady of Threadneedle Street like precision and was prudent to say the least with my credit card – drastic with the plastic just isn't my shopping bag.

Needless to say, during my divorce something happened to the grey matter and I couldn't quite do the sums as well as I used to. While going through my divorce I seemed to lose all ability to manage *anything* in all sorts of areas, with money becoming a particularly volatile minefield.

Everyone seemed to want something, or rather more accurately, money from me. Obviously I was paying the solicitor's bills for the divorce. I also had to pay a nanny to look after the boys so I had to increase her hours. She in turn increased her wages on a week-by-week basis, and as she was bigger than me and I had no family network to help me out – I paid up!

I also moved house and so had to meet all of those associated costs: removal vans, solicitors, insurance policies, etc … you name it, everything seemed to have a cost associated with it.

And, like so many others when they are suffering with divorce-mentia, I took to a few vices. Nothing too racy you understand. I've never been one to quaff vast quantities of alcohol and I didn't turn into a cocaine fiend either. But I did indulge in rather a lot of ciggies and reacted in a typical girlie way to trauma and went shopping. Oh dear, I made lots of mistakes there, most were never to see the light of day again from their hurled, screwed up positions at the back of my wardrobe.

I also made a huge and costly error with the mortgage. I stayed in the original family home for quite a period of time and I took over the mortgage in my sole name. But rather stupidly I hadn't looked into the implications of this. I just wanted everything straight as soon as possible and for life to take on some sort of normality. Bad move. In my haste, and without thinking things through properly, I was pretty much talked into anything. I said yes to more things than the man from Del Monte.

The upshot was that I took over a mortgage which meant that if I sold the property I would be liable for £7k worth of penalties. I was horrified to learn that it meant I would have to keep the mortgage until this penalty ran its course. Luckily it was portable, but I was saddled with this millstone mortgage for some time. I also had endowment payments linked with it and to be honest the whole thing baffled me.

Being a single mum, the finances were a major personal concern. What if I was made redundant? It's not like it hadn't happened to me before. Pity there's was no such thing as a job for life any more – rather like a marriage I remember wryly musing at the time.

If the worst-case scenario hit the fan, how would I pay the mortgage? What would happen to us? Sometimes the pressure to get it all right and keep all the plates spinning weighed heavy on my shoulders. Financial security became my overriding concern. Consequently, I saved like mad and made sure that on the new house I bought, I put a hefty deposit down and kept investing as much as my budget would allow. The rationale being that if the worst came to the worst, I could get a job that paid less money and still be able to afford to pay the bills.

One of the reasons I set up Restore was because I wanted to work with people, or partners as we call them, and be able to offer the advice I wish I had had then. Being able now to guide people through potentially one of the scariest times of their life and to advise them how not to be taken advantage of is incredibly rewarding. So if you're in spreadsheet hell at the moment I hope this chapter is of particular use to you too.

Independent financial advice

Financial advice – who needs it? As your life changes with things like divorce so do your financial needs.

Even if you have taken advice in the past, you may find out that what was right then may not be so ideal now. Even if you weren't thinking about it, you might be pleasantly surprised to discover how the right advice can improve the health of your finances.

When do you need advice?

It's important at every stage of your life. It's just as important that the advice keeps track as you get older and your concerns change. We've pointed out some of the issues and needs that you might consider.

How do I plan my finances?

Planning for a divorce can be done at any time. In times of emotional crisis it is often difficult to make well-thought-out decisions for the future. By planning you can help minimise what can be the crippling financial effects of the divorce. You can work out in advance how best to divide the income that formerly supported one home but which now must support two.

Frequently asked questions section

These are the most frequently asked questions in these circumstances.

1. How do I change my mortgage, as I don't think I can afford a house on my own now I no longer have a dual income?

There are a number of reasons you may want to change your mortgage, from moving house to removing an ex-partner or just getting a better deal. As with most areas of finance you need to talk to a specialist. A mortgage adviser will look at all sources of income you have i.e. salary, bonuses, maintenance payments, etc then they will try to find the best lender that suits your income and budget. These days many lenders will let you borrow high multiples of your income or even may not need proof of your income. You must remember, though, that interest rates are low at present and they can go up!

There are other options you could look at, like shared ownership, where you own part of the house and a housing association owns the remainder. This can cut your monthly costs.

2. What types of mortgages are there?

There are two main types of mortgage in common use. They are 'repayment' or 'interest only'. With a repayment mortgage you will pay some interest and some capital every month and by the end of the agreed term the full amount of the loan will have been repaid. This is a good method if you are cautious as it guarantees the loan will be repaid but it will not repay the loan early and it is not very flexible.

The other method, an interest only mortgage, is where you only pay interest every month to the lender so at the end of the term you still owe the full amount you have borrowed. You also run a savings plan alongside the mortgage and when this is worth the same amount as the outstanding debt you pay it off. This method has more risk as the savings play may not grow enough to clear the debt but if it performs well you can clear the debt early.

3. Are there companies who will provide mortgages for people on a low income?

Yes there are. As I mentioned in Q1 there are a number of options for people on lower incomes. You can look at lenders who will use high lending multiples of your income or at low start mortgages if your income will rise. It all depends on how much you want to borrow compared to the value of the house. The greater the percentage you borrow, the harder it is to place the mortgage.

The other option that is available is to use someone to be your guarantor. That means they will tell the lender that if you cannot pay the mortgage they guarantee that they will pay.

4. I am in debt; where can I go for help and advice?

A good place to start is with Citizens Advice Bureau who will point you in the right direction. It is also worth speaking to your financial adviser, as it is possible that they can save you a great deal of money with a re-mortgage. Also they may be able to help with debt consolidation.

5. Does being divorced prevent me from getting a mortgage or a loan?

If you are divorced you may be looking at buying out your ex-partner or buying a new place. There is no reason why you cannot get a mortgage but it is dependent on your income and how much you want to borrow. The best option is to speak to your adviser who will look at all of the best options for you.

6. What do I do about a pension as I was relying on my husband's?

Hopefully, as part of the divorce settlement your solicitor will have looked at pensions. The law has changed now to enable you to claim part of your ex-partner's pension as part of the settlement. You should also look at starting your own pension. If you are working then there is a good chance that you can start a pension via work. Company pensions are usually the best, as the company will contribute to them on your behalf. These days even people who do not work can have a pension. Speak to an adviser, who will give advice on how much you should be paying. Remember the sooner you start the less you will have to pay.

7. What special discounts or policies are available to me if I am divorced/widowed?

There are some discounts available on car insurance for single females but generally there are not discounts for those who are divorced or widowed. Life cover is also cheaper for ladies as they live longer but income protection is dearer for ladies as they are ill more often.

8. How can I secure my children's future if they want to go to University?

Funding for education is now getting to be very expensive since the introduction of tuition fees. This current cost also looks as if it will continue to rise as the government keep saying they are struggling to fund it. This all makes planning for higher education very difficult, as we do not know what amounts we will need to save. There are a number of ways you can save to fund education but generally they involve saving on a monthly basis or putting away lump sums. If you do some rough figures on what it would cost to send your child through University then speak to your adviser and they will give you the options. Again, to keep the costs down it is better to start while your children are very young.

9. Where do I find out about benefits that might be available to me?

Again, a good starting point is the CAB; they will give you the leaflets that are appropriate to your circumstances. Currently the family tax credit is an excellent help for families on low incomes.

10. How do I get more money out of my property without selling it?

This question is one of the most commonly asked because often one of the parties is looking to buy out the other as part of the divorce settlement. A re-mortgage is usually the best method to release some of the value of your property. These days the cash can be raised for almost any reason but putting the holiday, etc onto your mortgage means you will pay more interest in the longer term.

11. What are the financial implications if I move out of my house and rent it out and stay with someone else?

This type of situation can start to get complicated but the starting point should always be to tell your lender you are doing this. They may refuse you permission or they may charge you a higher rate of interest. If they refuse then you can look at a re-mortgage as there are lots of lenders that will allow you to then let. The next problem you may have is getting the rent out of your tenant and this is why you should look at using an agency to give you some security. You also can be liable for tax on the rent you receive. The other complication that can arise if you do not tell your lender you are letting the property this is sitters' rights, which can mean you lose control of the property. I suggest that this is an area where you definitely need to talk to your adviser.

12. How will my tax be affected now that I am divorce/widowed?

Generally it makes little difference these days as each individual has a basic tax allowance. There is also a married person's allowance but this only applies to people over 65. The tax relief that used to be on maintenance payments has also now finished for new cases. If you have specific queries then talk to your tax office, as they are now very helpful. If you have an estate valued at over £250,000 then you need to start to think about inheritance tax. There are lots of ways to reduce your tax bill and a good adviser will highlight these to you.

13. I have got a lump sum out of my settlement but I just have it in the building society. Is there a better way of maximising it?

Yes there is. Building society rates are very low at present and they are only just beating inflation. There are lots of ways to increase your return but they are dependent on how long you are prepared to put the money away for and how much risk you are prepared to take. The ideal solution is to start building a portfolio by spreading your money into a number of areas like stocks and shares, managed funds, with profits and cash. You also need to have the money split into short, medium and long-term investments. Always ensure you have enough funds available to cover emergencies. An adviser will match suitable investments to your specific needs.

14. How can I make my savings go further, to give me an income and a future lump sum?

As I said above, to get a better return you need to look at longer-term or higher-risk. An investment may look very good but ensure you read the small print, as often your capital will be at risk. There are a number of plans that will give an income but it depends on how much you need and what is your overall tax position. There are also some excellent guaranteed income plans on the market at present but a lot of these are only available for short periods. An adviser will try to build you a port-folio that will meet your income needs and ensure you also get some growth of your money. If you do not get any growth on your savings then they will start to fall in real value as inflation eats into them.

15. I am working and have a death-in-service policy but I don't have anything to protect me if I am ill or am unable to work.

It is a good start to have some cover at work. The first thing you should always look at with financial planning is protection. Life cover is the number one priority as there needs to be enough cash to enable some-one to look after your children in the event of your death.

A will is vital to designate someone to do this and hopefully you and your ex-partner have agreed on what would happen in this situation. You might find that in the event of ill health your employer will pay you. The standard pay is 6 months of full pay and 6 months at half pay. It can be a lot less than this. You should check with your employer and be very careful if they say it is at their discretion as it means they may not pay! There are a number of solutions and usually the best cover is obtained via an income protection policy. There are also accident, sickness and unemployment policies. The most suitable cover is dependent on how much cover you need, how old you are and what your medical history is. Your adviser will question you on these areas and recommend the most appropriate. Do not depend on the state as they have cut back on sick pay and you may find you only receive minimal support.

16. Where is the best place to put money at the moment to make the most of it?

Good question, but very difficult to answer. It is best to spread your money into different types of investments. If you have enough we always suggest a mix across all asset classes. That means cash, property, gilts and shares. It does depend on what your investment objectives are and your adviser will steer you in the right direction. The stock market is particularly low at present so stocks may look a good option but you must accept the risk that this type of investment offers.

17. What is an ISA and should I have one?

An ISA is an Individual Savings Account. As they are tax efficient then it is a good idea for most people. There are three types of ISA: cash, stocks and shares, and life assurance. You can put up to £7000 per year into ISAs. The cash option is the safest and should be part of most people's portfolio. If you top them up every year then you can build up a very nice tax-free pot of money, which could be used for things like education funding, special holidays, increasing your pension, etc.

18. Can I have an ISA in my children's name?

No, to hold an ISA you must be 18 years old. There are similar investments that can be held in your children's name if that is important to you.

19. Can I have a savings account in my children's name but use it myself?

Yes, you can have an account in a child's name and use it. Technically the fund must be for the benefit of the child as there are some tax benefits gained by putting money in their name. This area starts to get a bit cloudy as the tax office gets a bit uncomfortable with this. A child does have a full tax allowance and you can use this. I suggest this is definitely another area you need to talk to your adviser about.

20. I have an endowment mortgage with my ex-husband. Now I have the house should I cash this in and release the cash?

No, the endowment will normally form part of the settlement and it is best to keep it going if possible. We always suggest it is best to keep the endowment, as the cash-in value will rarely be as high as the amount you have paid in. Try to agree who is going to keep the policy and transfer the ownership into one name. There are other options that also may be better than cashing it in. It is possible to sell your plan to a specialist who will often pay more than the surrender value. If you still have a mortgage then use the plan to repay part of the mortgage. Just make sure that the plan is still on target to repay the loan at maturity.

21. I cannot afford a repayment but am unsure about endowment mortgages due to the bad press; what should I do?

The cost difference between the two methods is usually very similar. If you want to guarantee your mortgage is paid off at the end of the term then a repayment is best for you. If you would like the possibility of clearing your loan early then an endowment is best for you. You must be prepared to accept the extra risk that it may not have grown enough to clear all of the debt. Also, endowments are generally more flexible and can be moved with the mortgage. If you go down the endowment route then make sure you review the growth of the plan every five years to ensure it is on track to clear the debt.

22. I don't have a pension; how do I go about getting one?

If you are working then the first step is to speak to your employer. The pension legislation now states that any company with over five employees must offer access to a pension scheme. If you are not working you can still do a stakeholder pension. There is a limit on how much you can put in, which is currently £3600 per year. You can also use an ISA to plan for your retirement. The priority is to get a tax-effective way that meets your future needs. Any good adviser will tell you all of the options.

23. Is it worth getting a pension if I am only working part time?

Yes, as we believe the real value of the state pension will start to fall in the future, so you need to provide for yourself. You can start a pension with as little as £20 per month. This will not give you enough to live on at retirement but it is a start. You can then increase your contributions as you have more spare cash. You can also put lump sums into a pension if you have any spare cash.

24. How do I get a pension and which are the best ones to go for?

As I have already discussed, there are lots of types of pension available and it all depends on your individual circumstances. If you talk to your adviser they will steer you in the right direction.

25. My ex-husband and I have a business in our joint names; what happens financially now we are apart?

I suggest you speak to a solicitor or an accountant for accurate information.

Buying your home

You may, like me, decide that you cannot really stay in the former family home. This may be due to the financial circumstances you now find yourself in or because you feel as if the house holds too many memories and too many impressions of the old you. For whatever reason, you may find your new situation daunting, particularly if you have only bought property when you were with your partner.

The financial partners that we use on our programmes are Bradford & Bingley and they have always been so helpful to our clients, genuinely nice people to work with. And as they are the largest UK independent financial advisers they know what they are talking about.

They have worked with Restore to produce this easy to follow guide on the steps to remember when branching out into a new home on your own. The first time I walked into my new 'single parent' home it had a lovely, safe, family feeling and I truly loved that house; it represented stability, security, safeness, a new start, family – all sorts of feelings come to mind. I am glad I moved house, some of my friends chose not to and were then upset when their ex-husbands still treated the property as if they still lived there, some still even had keys. I wanted my house to be mine and the kids: something which was no longer part of that old relationship or family.

Tips for finding your ideal home

LOCATION, LOCATION, LOCATION. It doesn't matter how attractive a property may be, it's situation is critical. If you aren't already familiar with the area, spend some time getting to know about it by asking friends or your potential neighbours.

It's worthwhile trying to stay in the same location, if possible, for the support network you have built up. I was initially going to move to a different area but felt the change would be too much for me and the kids so we moved to where they could still see their friends and so could I and their schools did not change.

THINK OF YOUR FUTURE. Will the property you have your eye on still meet your needs a few years from now? Will your compact and cosy home turn into a cramped one? Will your children be able to grow up happily and safely?

PEACE AND QUIET. If you've viewed the property at the weekend, check the roads nearby at busier times. The last thing you'll want is your peace spoilt by fume-laden, noisy traffic.

RUNNING COSTS. Take a moment to consider the running costs. Old houses are usually more expensive to heat than modern ones. Ask to see the heating bills for the previous four quarters so you know what you're letting yourself in for.

How much can you borrow?

Before you start looking for a house it pays to find out exactly how much you can borrow. This will save you setting your heart on a home that may cost more than you can afford.

How much you can borrow isn't always the same as how much you should borrow. Usually lenders will lend a single person around three times their annual income (before tax). With couples it's usually three times the larger income plus one times the other or two and a half times the joint income – whichever suits you better.

If you borrow as much as you can it's worth keeping in mind how this might affect your lifestyle. (Later in this section we have included a budget section, which will help you see how much you need to live on according to your current needs.)

How much interest will you pay?

You'll be charged interest on the amount you borrow. The Bank of England sets a basic interest rate (the base rate) and your lender will charge you a rate that relates to this.

The rate goes up and down in response to economic conditions. If your mortgage is on a variable rate, you usually pay less when rates come down and more when they go up.

Some lenders adjust your payments in the month the base rate changes; others adjust the payments annually.

Make sure your lender alters your payments in the way that suits you best.

Interest rates and the amount you borrow

The type of mortgage deal you are offered often depends on what's called the loan to value ratio – which means how much you need to borrow compared to the value of your property. If you put a larger deposit on the house, you may get a better deal than if you borrowed more from the lender.

Different types of mortgage deals

If your mortgage is on a variable rate, your monthly payments will vary. To avoid this in the initial period you can opt for a fixed rate or capped rate mortgage. A fixed rate means you pay the same for the first few years regardless of what the base rate is doing.

Fixed rates give you peace of mind and help you to plan your finances early on. But do remember that a fixed rate that looks good now may not be so attractive if the base rate goes a long way down.

That's why capped rate mortgages are often popular – where the rates can't rise above a certain set interest rate but you benefit if the base rate falls.

Another option is a discounted rate, where for a set period the rate you pay undercuts the lender's normal rate – but still goes up and down with the base rate.

Some mortgages (fixed and variable) give cash back at the start – useful to cover moving costs or to pay your solicitor and valuation fees. With some mortgage lenders these fees are also paid for you as part of the deal.

There is also a new type of mortgage called a Tracker Mortgage, which is linked to the Bank of England base rate. So whenever the bank rate falls or rises, your mortgage will follow, up or down, by a set amount.

The deals that are often suitable for people buying their first home on their own are:

- Fixed rate – because you can plan your finances and are protected from rate changes for the first few years.
- Discounted rate – because you can benefit from lower payments at the start.
- Capped rate – because you can be sure of the maximum payments during the first few years.

As a first time buyer you will also probably benefit from special mortgage deals. You need to check that there are no strings attached but lenders tend to offer these to first time buyers to help them off to a good start.

Ways to repay your mortgage

Once you've decided how much you want to pay back each month, it's time to get advice on the best way to repay your mortgage. There are lots of different mortgage combinations, but they can be split into two main options:

- Repayment: You pay off some of the loan every month – so the amount you owe decreases over time. Obviously you pay interest too – the two amounts are added together and you make one overall monthly payment. It means that every year you owe slightly less than the year before until you've paid off the whole amount you originally borrowed.
- Interest only: You only pay interest on the amount you've borrowed – not the loan itself – until the end of the mortgage term. You must then repay this in one go. In order to do this you should also pay another amount each month into a separate investment fund. The idea is that at the end of the mortgage your investment will have grown to match what you owe – and this is used to pay off your

mortgage. If the investment has performed well there may be some left over for you, but if the investment growth has been poor you will have to make up the difference yourself. There are a number of different investments you can choose to repay your mortgage. Your adviser will help you to find the best one for you.

There are two main ways to repay an interest-only mortgage:	
Endowment	You pay a fixed amount every month into an endowment policy with an insurance company. Usually your premium goes into a fund, which is reinvested for you on the stock market. The idea is that at the end of your mortgage term it should have grown enough to pay off your loan. Endowments also provide build-in-life cover to pay off your mortgage if you die before the end of the repayment term.
ISA (Individual Savings Account)	ISAs are a tax-efficient way of saving. Usually these are through a unit trust, which is a fund of investments run by professional investment managers. Your money buys units in the fund, which you hope will increase in value. ISAs do not include life cover so you have to arrange your own.

A word of warning – one thing to remember about these methods is that THE LEVEL OF YOUR INVESTMENTS MAY GO DOWN AS WELL AS UP. The ISA or endowment policy will be managed on your behalf by experts to give the best return. They will keep you informed on a regular basis about how your investments are doing and whether they are growing fast enough.

The idea is that the value of your fund should grow to a level that will allow you to pay off the amount you have borrowed. There may even be some left over for you to keep and spend as you like – but this is never guaranteed.

If the fund doesn't grow fast enough, or there is a drop in the value of the stock market, you may need to find the balance from elsewhere.

Early surrender may have adverse financial consequences – for example, not producing enough funds to repay the mortgage loan.

How do you pick the right investment for you?
You will need to consider charges, the level of risk involved, flexibility

of the contract and the combination of benefits available – so you will need expert advice to find the right one for you.

Life assurance

Whatever the type of mortgage you have, you will need to protect your family or others left behind if you die before the end of your mortgage term.

Endowment policies and some pension mortgages will have built-in life cover. This means that they pay what you owe if you die before the mortgage term is up. If you have a repayment mortgage you will need to buy the life insurance separately.

1) Term assurance pays a fixed amount if you die (in this case the amount you borrow) within a set number of years (usually the mortgage term).
2) Whole-of-life cover has no set term.

There are many different types of term and whole-of-life insurance and they can vary enormously in value. Once more, independent financial advice can help you find the best insurance for your needs.

Other things to think about

Mortgages can be complicated and can sometimes include hidden extras that you will have to pay for. It is therefore important you have this fully explained to you before you enter into your mortgage. As part of the service the adviser should look at charges levied by different lenders and explain exactly what you will pay for the mortgage they eventually recommend. The main ones to look out for are:

MORTGAGE VALUATION. Your mortgage lender will require a valuation of the property they're lending on to know if it provides suitable security for the loan. The cost of a mortgage valuation depends on the value of the property and is usually paid for by you. There are two other valuation services that provide more details and give you, the purchaser, more information about the property.

HOMEBUYER SURVEY AND VALUATION. This combines a basic mortgage valuation with a more detailed guide to the condition of the property and the valuer or the surveyor's opinion of its value in the open market.

It's particularly good if you are short of time and looking for a well-priced option.

STRUCTURAL/BUILDING SURVEY. This is the most detailed and informative survey you can have. It's based on a thorough examination of the property and provides in-depth information, covering the property's condition, any structural faults and any other problems.

HIGH LOAN TO VALUE FEE. First time buyers usually need to borrow more, which means they may be charged a high loan to value fee. The 'loan' is simply the amount you are borrowing. The 'value' is the purchase price or the property value, whichever is lower. It's a term usually expressed as a percentage so if, for example, you want to borrow £75,000 and the property value is £100,000, the loan to value will be 75%.

A fee is usually charged when the loan to value exceeds 75%. The lender arranges Mortgage Indemnity Guarantee Insurance to protect itself if the borrower can't make all the mortgage repayments, but the borrower remains liable for the full mortgage debt.

LEGAL SERVICES. Your solicitor or licensed conveyancer will charge a fee (usually a few hundred pounds) and then make various payments on your behalf that you'll have to reimburse including:

- Stamp Duty – This is the Government's one-off 'purchase tax' on all properties above a certain value. Your solicitor or licensed conveyancer will collect this and pass it on – so even if your legal fees are being paid, you will still need to find the money for this.
- Land registration and local search fees – the charge for your solicitor or licensed conveyancer to confirm exactly what the seller owns and for a local authority search to confirm, for example, that there are no major building or road schemes planned near your home. Also includes fees for registering your ownership at the land registry.

INSURANCE. Buildings insurance safeguards your property against a variety of possible accidents or damage. You must have a buildings insurance policy to provide security on the mortgage loan. You may, however, be required by the lender to take out a compulsory insurance, depending on the deal you eventually choose.

Contents insurance covers the possessions within your home such as your furniture, your valuables and your personal belongings. Buildings and contents can be covered by a single policy.

Payment Protection insurance covers your repayments if you cannot work because you fall ill or are made redundant.

HOUSEHOLD BILLS. Don't forget about these. Most of the gas, water and electricity companies require some payment in advance. Then there's council tax, telephone, TV licence, cable television – the list goes on.

OTHER CHARGES. There may be additional charges associated with buying a mortgage, including arrangement or client fees.

What happens next?

You have found the perfect home. What do you do now?

MAKING THE OFFER. You make your offer to the estate agent. If accepted, you should instruct your solicitor and provide their details to your estate agent. You should also contact your mortgage adviser to apply for a mortgage.

AGREEING THE CONTRACT. Your solicitor will negotiate and agree the contract. The solicitor will check the documentation to establish exactly what the seller owns and will make searches and enquiries of the local authority to ensure you don't have any nasty surprises upon completion.

EXCHANGING CONTRACTS. Once contracts are agreed, your solicitor will ask you to sign the contract. The seller will sign the contract on an identical form and your solicitor will arrange for contracts to be exchanged. On exchange a deposit, normally 10% or sometimes 5% of the purchase price, will be payable.

COMPLETION. On completion your solicitor will arrange for the price (less the deposit) to be paid and in return you will get the keys to your new home. Your solicitor will arrange to register your ownership at the land registry subject to the mortgage.

ARE THERE ANY OTHER CHARGES? There will be other charges and you will need to check with your adviser what these are likely to be, usually a fee set by your chosen lender, valuation and solicitor's fees and possibly additional fees from your adviser.

Your step-by-step guide

The following flow chart gives a more detailed outline of each stage and explains how you can speed up the process. It illustrates the step-by-step home buying process, and how long you can reasonably expect to wait for things to happen at each stage (although, with home buying nothing is ever set in stone).

Please note that, where a telephone is indicated, you are advised to chase up whichever party is holding up the process, as delays are virtually inevitable. Never be afraid of contacting your estate agent, solicitor or mortgage adviser at any given stage: they are there to ensure that your home buying procedure goes ahead smoothly and with a minimum of fuss, and they should do just that.

Mortgage Code

There is a voluntary Mortgage Code, which some advisers follow and those advisers will hold a copy at their branches.

Mortgage terms and their meanings

The following are a list of terms you will come across when reading about mortgages:

- **APR:** Annual Percentage Rate of interest charged on the loan, used as a means of comparing the cost of credit. It includes interest and charges and takes into account any fixed or discounted rates of interest. It is calculated in accordance with regulations made under the Consumer Credit Act.
- **Agent:** A local representative of the Company, usually an accountant, solicitor or estate agent.
- **Base rate:** The standard rate of interest charged for borrowing money. It rises or falls broadly in line with the rate set by the Bank of England.
- **Buildings insurance:** Insurance against damage to the structure of the building such as the roof. It excludes contents in the house. Most lenders require this to be taken out.
- **Capital:** The lump sum of money lent to you to pay the seller of the

house you are buying. Alternatively it may be used to pay another lender if you're moving your mortgage. Interest is charged on the capital.

- **Capped rate:** An interest rate set for a period of time that can vary, but cannot rise above a certain pre-agreed limit.
- **Cash back:** A payment you might receive from the lender when you take out a mortgage. It may be a fixed amount or a percentage of the amount of the mortgage. This is usually offered instead of a capped, discounted or fixed rate and therefore you pay interest at the lender's standard variable rate.
- **Contents insurance:** Insurance that covers items inside your home, for example, your possessions, furniture and carpets, against damage and burglary, etc. It's optional but highly recommended.
- **Conveyancing:** The legal process involved in buying and selling property.
- **Deeds:** The paperwork that gives the holder ownership of the house. Deeds are held by the mortgage lender until the mortgage is repaid.
- **Discounted rate:** A guaranteed rate lower than the lender's standard variable mortgage base rate. This often lasts for an agreed period, usually the first few years.
- **Endowment:** A life insurance policy, into which you pay a set sum for a certain number of years. The aim is that at the end of your mortgage term it should have grown enough to pay off your loan. Endowments also provide built-in life cover to pay off your mortgage if you die before the end of the repayment term. There are different types of endowment: 'with profit', 'unit linked' and 'unitised with profits'. Please note, if investment growth is less than the planned assumed growth rate, a shortfall in the amount required to repay the loan may occur when the policy matures.
- **Fixed rate:** A set rate of interest charged on a mortgage over an agreed period of time, usually the first few years.
- **Freehold:** This is when you own the property (house) and the land it is situated on.
- **FSA (Financial Services Authority):** The single regulatory body, which monitors the companies and individuals who offer financial advice.
- **Income protection:** An insurance policy that guarantees to replace your income should you become unable to earn a living. It will always be subject to conditions and exclusions.
- **Interest-only mortgage:** A mortgage where you make monthly re-

payments of interest only and repay the capital at the end of the mortgage term. It is advisable to take out an investment plan such as endowment, ISA or pension to assist you to repay the capital at the end.

- **Interest rate:** The rate at which interest is charged on the money you borrow.
- **Independent Financial Advice:** An Independent Financial Adviser (IFA) will select products from the whole marketplace and is able to offer the widest choice. This applies to endowments, ISAs, pensions and other stock market related investments, not to the mortgage itself.
- **Individual Savings Accounts (ISAs):** The Government introduced the tax-free Individual Savings Account (ISA) as a replacement to the popular Personal Equity Plan (PEP) in the hope that it would encourage more people to save money. Launched on 6 April 1999, the ISA scheme is guaranteed to run for at least 10 years. In many ways, it can be seen as a successor to both TESSAs and PEPs, bringing both cash savings and stock market based investments into the scope of one scheme. An ISA consists of up to three parts – cash, insurance and stocks and shares. Each part has its own annual investment limit.
- **Leasehold:** This is when you own the property for a number of years, after which it goes back to the freeholder. Flats are usually leasehold. Most lenders will also lend on leasehold properties but will require there to be a number of years left on the lease before making a loan.
- **Life assurance:** An insurance policy on the life of the other person. A benefit is payable in the event of death. It is advisable to take out life assurance in conjunction with a mortgage for an amount sufficient to cover the outstanding debt.
- **Loan to Value (LTV):** The size of your mortgage as a percentage of the value of the property or the price paid for the property.
- **Mortgage:** This word is commonly used to describe a loan secured on your property. This security will remain in existence until the loan is paid off.
- **Mortgage Indemnity Guarantee (MIG):** An insurance policy that covers the lender if your property is repossessed and the lender cannot get the money back from you. You are charged a MIG if you borrow over a certain loan to value percentage, usually 75%, to cover the cost of this insurance.

- **Negative equity:** This is where the value of your property is less than the outstanding balance on your mortgage.
- **Payment Protection Insurance:** An insurance policy that pays your monthly instalments in the event of accident, sickness or unemployment. It will always be subject to conditions and exclusions.
- **Pension (Personal or Stakeholder):** This is an option if you don't have a company pension scheme. When taken out in conjunction with a mortgage the aim is that at the time of repaying the loan there should be enough to pay off your mortgage and hopefully leave some for your pension. Life cover can be included.
- **Repossession:** This is the last remedy, if the borrower is unable to pay the monthly mortgage instalments. The mortgage lender may have to sell the home to recover the money owed on it.
- **Repayment mortgage:** A mortgage where you pay off some of the capital and some of the interest on the loan each month.
- **Security:** Something that is held by a lender until a loan is repaid, usually a mortgage on a property. It may also be a guarantee or the assignment of a life policy.
- **Stamp duty:** A tax you pay on the transfer of property. Only people borrowing over a certain amount or living in a certain area have to pay this.
- **Structural survey:** A thorough examination of the property, which should reveal material faults. It is optional and you must pay the cost of the survey. It provides protection for you as a potential buyer because of the information it gives.
- **Tracker mortgage:** A type of mortgage that is linked to the Bank of England base rate. So whenever the base rate falls or rises your mortgage will follow it up or down by a set amount.
- **Vacating fee:** A charge made by the lender when you repay the mortgage.
- **Valuation:** This is the most basic valuation service and assesses how much the property is worth and whether it is suitable security. It is usually carried out by the lender on their behalf but you may receive a copy of the report.
- **Variable rate:** An interest rate that goes up and down in line with the lender's standard mortgage base rate. Your payments change accordingly.

4 *Flying solo*

*Sometimes it is less hard to wake up feeling lonely when you are
alone than wake up feeling lonely when you are with someone.*

LIV ULLMAN

Before we enter that minefield on flirting, dating and relationships, let's tarry a while in singledom. Yes, that very place where the Bridget Joneses and 'men behaving badly' of this world hang out.

Once you've got over, or at least are coming to terms with, the sting of relationship fallout, going solo is really not such a bad state to be in – really it's not. Obviously, you don't want to hang around in this situation like an unclaimed piece of left luggage for too long but never underestimate the value of spending a few months alone.

The reasons are more than valid. Think about it. It may have been years since you were not someone else's other half. You may have completely lost sight of who you were, what makes you tick and why. It might be a cliché, but taking time out to discover yourself is time well spent.

Women in particular are masters at the art of accommodating other people's wishes. You will have changed since you got married, even if the passage of time hasn't changed you, what you have gone through probably has.

Then, emotions aside, there are other benefits to being master of your own destiny. Think back to all those times he hogged the TV remote, or she made you sit through her boxed collection of Sex in the City videos. Think of all those three-course business dinners you don't have to cook any more to impress his boss, when all along you used to salivate over the supermarket deep freezer at the thought of all those delicious ready to serve meals for one.

Men – no more polite afternoon teas at her mother's when you could be watching Ski Sunday or going to the races. Divorce is so civilised in a way because you can renounce that whole cast of in-laws – if you want to.

Your money is your own, so no more summit meetings just to decide on whether it's Chinese takeaway or a pizza delivery. Your time is your own to allocate how you want to – you are your own boss, remember.

You can hog the duvet and lie like a starfish if you want and no one is going to lay a guilt trip on you in the morning for doing so.

So, book yourself a ticket for any concert your ex would have refused to go to. Indulge yourself in any a treat, outing, weekend break or holiday that takes your fancy, *simply because you can*. And that's the only reason you need.

One of my friends/clients took great pleasure in making a hair appointment to have her hair coloured dark brown, which was her natural colour. Why? Because throughout her marriage her ex-husband preferred her being a bleached blonde.

In her excellent book *Shortcuts to bouncing back from heartbreak*, personal development trainer, Gael Lindenfield gives this excellent advice on being on your own. She recommends giving yourself two special periods of solitude every week, like treating yourself to a delicious café latte and the newspapers in a coffee shop where others are obviously enjoying their own space and time. Or time spent perusing an art gallery all by yourself in perfect peace. The point of the exercise is to have positive experiences of time alone and it soon becomes something to be valued and enjoyed, not feared or regarded as negative 'failure' time.

Self-esteem and thinking positively

Besides, if you're the one that has been left, your self-esteem may have plunged lower than a lift shaft, and that will need time to build up. And slowly but surely your self-confidence will come trickling back. You'll find that you need precious time on your own to work on areas like self-esteem, confidence and learning to think positively, so now is the time to do it. Believe me on this one – time to yourself is always time well spent. And besides, how can you ever get to know and love someone else unless you know and love yourself first? As Oscar Wilde said, 'To love oneself is to conduct a lifelong love affair.'

People with high self-esteem have a positive outlook on life. Thinking positively can be worked on; it's a mental exercise whereby you literally push away the barriers of negative thinking.

Helen Hale, a Life Coach who lectures on various Restore programmes, states that you need to reverse negative thinking with positive. Most of our thoughts are negative and they are coming directly from within. She makes the excellent point that we spend the majority of our time with the very person who should be our best friend – ourselves. Yet this alleged best friend is possibly the most critical person we know. How many times do you look in the mirror and criticise your own appearance? How many times do you tell yourself that you could never achieve a task? Would you really want a friend in your life who was so destructive to your own self-worth?

Get into the habit of telling yourself you are lovely, capable, talented and strong. Every time you achieve a task you've never tackled before give yourself a mental pat on the back. When things aren't going so well, don't go to pieces. But do take an affirmative stroll down Memory Lane, remind yourself of all your successes and tell yourself that you can pull this off successfully too. You may have to wait for the right moment or energy level but you will do it. Just as you have before.

Don't let doubters get to you but use them as incentives to achieve what they think you can't.

Be assertive. You don't have to be a victim, you are only one by choice. Learn to state what you want, and think what's best for you.

Sometimes we have to adapt our style to suit the situation, so learn how to do this. Always be willing and open to hear the other person's side and settle for compromise if a stalemate seems likely.

If you've been hurt it's very easy to close yourself down so that you don't risk having your feelings pulverized as they were before. Unfortunately, as understandable as this is, it blocks you from receiving positive and learning experiences too. So try to relax, don't let the past cloud your present and avoid being too prickly to approach. Allow yourself to be motivated by others, i.e. people whose values and opinions you trust.

So once you have trained yourself to think positively you can work on building up your self-esteem, which pretty much goes hand in hand anyway so you will have done a lot of the ground work already. A really good way is to join a course. At this stage of the game anything that takes you out of yourself and gets you meeting a cross-section of people and teaches you life skills is a total bonus – so get your name down. (You'll find details of my Restore courses at the back of the book!)

People with high self-esteem are always reminding themselves of their successes in life. One of my clients' favourite self-help sayings is, 'If I can do it once, I can do it again.' She applies this to all the tasks that she finds daunting because it's a reminder to her that she did successfully sit 16 people down to dinner without a hitch. She did decorate her sitting room worthy of a Home Front programme and she did pick herself up after yet another doomed love affair while laughing at the good bits and learning from the not so good parts.

Self-confidence, not to be confused with arrogance of course, is that lovely happy, shining quality that some lucky people effortlessly have. It's not only wonderful to possess but it is a very attractive trait and naturally draws people to you.

Watch and learn from those you know who just have that X factor – and the best thing about it is that it's socially contagious – a bug you do want to get. What you will note is that confident people tend to make rational, informed decisions; they are cool and calculated risk takers. They leave the past firmly behind them and they don't dwell on mistakes but simply juice out what there was to learn and then, fuss free, they move on. They are past masters at positive thinking. Over the years they have honed their gut feelings so that they can trust their instincts and they have an uncanny knack of knowing that what they are doing, thinking, saying and planning is right. That way they don't allow people without their sense of self to sway any of their decisions. Should they find they have made the wrong decision or miscalculated they adapt to the situation quickly, re-group and *get on with it*. You'll never find one of these people in the company of the hand wringers of this world.

Needless to say, self-confident people travel light through life – lugging around emotional baggage simply isn't their style. It doesn't mean that they've put their feelings into cold storage, it simply means they recognise that when it's over, it's over. The fat lady sang, the curtain came down and the audience went home. The end.

And so with your esteem riding high, your self-confidence nicely buffed up, and all those nagging doubts about your future silenced through lots of positive thinking, you are now ready to leap into the dating pool. Let's go for it!

5   *Dating*

> *A girl can wait for the right man to come along, but in the meantime, that still doesn't mean she can't have a wonderful time with all the wrong ones.*
>
> CHER

When it comes to style, by rights I should still be serving time for breaking just about every rule in the fashion book the first time I went out clubbing after splitting from my ex.

So, the fashionistas out there look away now while I described just what I was wearing and remember I simply wasn't used to the dating scene.

There that's me, not quite in the spotlight but freakily picked out in the strobe lighting. I wore one of my work skirts, flesh coloured tights, a sparkly sequined top and my hair scrapped back in a bun. Hot? I think not! The only person I talked to that night was a man who was orthodontically challenged and wearing an orange toupee. And because I didn't know how to handle the occasion I ended up giving him my phone number! Ridiculous, but sadly true.

I also went through a stage of 'divorce puberty'. That's where you go back to a particular reference point when you were young and in the early days of dating. A lot of my fashion purchases then were shockers. I particularly remember a pair of leather trousers I spent a fortune on. I was too underweight for them so they hung off me like flabby hide and I looked like I was ready for the knackers' yard!

Tips for the ladies

The moral of the story is this – before you hit the dating scene properly, first go out on a couple of dry runs with a posse of trusted mates. Check out what everyone is wearing so that you feel comfortable with your image. Learn to handle your alcohol intake and remember the following advice:

- Don't hand your telephone number out willy nilly.
- Don't be coerced into going on dates that you don't want to.
- Don't go back to a total stranger's house and have unprotected sex.
- Don't give away personal details until you are absolutely sure you do want the cutie in corner to know how many times you took your driving test before you passed, your blood group, and more importantly *really* personal details like how many children you've got and where you live.
- Don't look desperate. Nothing is more off putting than someone with a 'puppy dog/love me, love me, please!' expression on their face.

And, more mature ladies, don't borrow your teenage daughter's crop tops, mini skirts or thigh-high patent leather boots in the hope that as it's dark no one will clock your age. They will. Looking like hot mutton will put the average decent bloke off. You will, however, attract every letch for miles around.

You are a woman now, not a girl, so behave and dress like one. Believe me, the classy Mrs Robinsons in the dating league tables are scoring just as well and in some cases better than their younger counterparts.

Men are visual creatures for sure. But most men, decent ones I mean, love a woman who can carry on a conversation, smiles a lot but not so much that you might think she was auditioning for the part as the village idiot, is pleasant and conveys a natural warm personality. Even better if she has high self-esteem, but is obviously not a ball breaker and definitely not the type to seize his heart and crack it over her bended knee while shouting, 'NEXT!'

Of course they would all like to date Britney Spears or any of the female cast of Hollyoaks, but for most men, being the fairly realistic souls they are, meeting a female with all the above attributes will do nicely.

Tips for the men

Likewise men:

- Don't over do the sun bed and end up looking like tan man.

- Don't come out with any ridiculous chat-up lines.
- Don't dress like your teenage son – hot ram just doesn't do it for the average gal.
- Watch the amount of gold chains, ear rings and rings. Discreet jewellery is fine, but 'yer on my manor' knuckle-dusters – no thanks.
- Don't overdo hair gel, mousse and aftershave. We don't want to fear we will be competing for bathroom shelf space.

And watch your shoes. They are a dead give away as to your personality type apparently. Some girls swear that whatever you've got on your feet will predict what your character, hobbies and interests are likely to be and therefore whether it will be worth their while accepting your kind offer of half a lager or not.

Also, make sure that as far as humanly possible you have ditched a lot of emotional junk. Not all men are bastards; not all women are bitches. Dump the junk and you'll find that you are more than ready to receive lots of new experiences.

This next point is really worth remembering. It's a tough one to get your head round, let alone your heart, but I can't help agreeing with John Gray of *Men are from Mars, Woman are from Venus* fame when he wrote, 'When we are upset, 90 per cent of the upset is related to our past and has nothing to do with what we think is upsetting us. Generally only about 10 per cent of our upset is appropriate to the present situation.' So just keep the past in perspective.

Bearing all that in mind, we all know that the best way to get over someone is to go forth and find someone else!

Flirting

I organise several different courses within the Restore programmes. One of them is titled, Right Start After a Divorce. Throughout it we look at all the areas to do with rebuilding your self-confidence and taking greater control of your life.

I am going to include some tips for 'flirting' but my perspective is that flirting is unnecessary. How do I work that one out? Well, think about it, it's like seeing a beautifully packaged present under the tree with tinsel, bright papers and ribbons and then, when you unwrap it, inside there is a tiny bar of soap – it's a bit of a let down really isn't it?

When we work on our confidence and work on ourselves, spending time understanding what we want, what motivates us and what makes us happy, we naturally feel better, more confident, stronger and so we naturally attract people to us. The problem that I see with 'learning how to flirt' is that all we learn to do is mask ourselves, working on making someone else feel good so that they are attracted to us. But surely they are just attracted to the signals and to who they think we are?

In my experience, and that of my clients, when you come out of a crisis such as a divorce you feel very needy and vulnerable and so to go out and practise these 'flirting skills' means that you tend to attract the wrong sort of people. Like attracts like, so vulnerable people attract vulnerable and needy people. I see this all the time and my advice is to ignore all those books on how to flirt, and read those that teach you how to communicate more effectively and how to really develop your listening skills. Learn to make yourself happy first and then you will automatically attract the right sort of people into your life – trust me I am living proof of someone who cannot flirt to save their life! To this day, if you ask any of my friends (even my oldest friends from my teenage days) they will tell you that flirting was not exactly my speciality but I have managed to meet and marry someone.

However, I also realise that not all of you are going to believe me, so here are some not altogether serious tips on how to flirt, provided by one of our Life Coaches:

Men – simple and straightforward – it just takes courage; but remember not too much of the Dutch variety.

- Catch the eye of whoever has taken your fancy – in a non-threatening way; *don't stare* whatever you do.
- Smile and think warm thoughts; that way your expression shows in your eyes and makes them twinkle.
- Stand tall and adopt a non-defensive posture.
- If the object of your desire meets your gaze and smiles, glances away but returns to meet your look again – hey presto! You're in with a good chance.
- So give a little nod of acknowledgement and move in for a chat.
- As nerve-wracking as it is, try to make her laugh. I don't mean you have to mount a vaudeville act worthy of A Night at the London

Palladium, but anything that raises a smile goes down well in the female world.

- And for goodness' sake don't muscle in with any controversial subjects unless of course your name happens to be Jeremy Paxman.

Girls, you're probably not aware of it but you are putting out the majority of the flirting signals in a non-verbal way already. However, you can help yourself.

- Smile – big wide open ones that light up the eyes.
- Whatever you do – do it with enthusiasm – men love animated girls who look like they'd be really good company, but don't overdo it.
- Once you've chosen your quarry, send out short darting looks at him. Look away and then look back quickly.
- Chances are, if they like you, they are mirroring your actions too – if so, swiftly turn to your girly mates and mouth as subtly as you can, 'don't worry about me I've got my taxi fare home, text you tomorrow.'
- While you maintain eye contact, toss your hair or run your fingers through your tresses.
- Once you are certain you have made a favourable impression, step up the signals like nodding your head in his direction, fluttering your eyelashes, putting your shoulders back and pushing your breasts forward. There! If that doesn't do it he's probably gay. But if you can clearly see that his tongue is hanging out and his pupils are so dilated that you can't even tell what colour his eyes actually are, then don't waste a second. Invite him to take a seat, lick your lips in that sexy anticipatory way and wait to be charmed as he threads his way man- fully towards you.
- Ladies, do be kind and generous of spirit. Have you any idea how much courage it has taken him to walk that walk across to where you are sitting and face possible rejection *and* under the scrutiny of his mates.
- Now the next few minutes could be crucial. How you come across may depend on whether you carry this meeting on to swapping tel- ephone numbers or even further – to *a real date*. You never get a second chance to make a first impression remember.

Men, do now offer to buy the lady a drink. I can't impress upon you how we girls love generosity. But, a word of caution for both of you in these date rape drug times. Go to the bar together then, girls, you know your drink hasn't been tampered with and, blokes, you are above suspicion.

OK, all joking aside, if you really feel that you want to go out and 'nab a man', or woman, then I am sure this sort of thing may be useful to you, in moderation. But don't get hung up on it. If you have been married for a long time what's being single for a couple of months or even years going to do? It's not going to hurt you to spend that time with good friends, starting hobbies, going on holidays and learning about yourself. There are so many people in the world that the law of averages says you will meet someone, so why rush it?

Where to meet your match and what you might expect

Pubs and clubs

A good and obvious choice you might think and indeed there has been many a match struck in a pub, absolutely no pun intended.

It's a better choice than a club venue because chatting volume is usually far more easily achievable and if you make one or two pubs your local or regular hang out, you can get to know who's who and, of equal importance, who is eligible or not.

The nightclub is a great place to go if you want to polish up your flirting techniques but best played only for fun. Being realistic this isn't the recommended happy hunting ground for meaningful relationships to take root and blossom. Nearly everyone will be alcohol fuelled and the blokes will be so high on Dutch courage they could probably capture Saddam Hussein single handed, or at least think they could. By going home time your vision may well be impaired and your senses certainly will be. So go have a good time by all means and leave all your expectations safely at home.

Dating agencies

Worth a whirl but again I think it's rather hit and miss. They don't have the stigma they used to as so many people of all ages and careers are applying to go on their books. Good for the cash-rich but time-poor folk – who simply can't fit a love life or rather the ground work into their hectic lifestyles. Or if you find getting out to meet people tricky because you live in a remote area for instance or you have children.

Shop around for an agency that has the type of clientele most likely to suit your 'would like to meet' list. And do observe the 'how to rendez-vous' safety guidelines.

Online

Entertaining perhaps but wide open to misuse. The watchword here is don't believe everything you read on your screen or that beams from a chatroom somewhere out in cyberspace.

Potential suitors could be as innocent as the Internet is wide but don't be naïve. One man from Scotland was hopelessly taken in by a woman claiming to be an exotic, half Apache Red Indian beauty. He fell in love with her image and her sweet talk on screen and on the telephone. On the strength of his feelings he sold his home, left his job and flew out to meet his sweetie. Unfortunately she turned out to be a bored, lonely and depressed housewife from Wisconsin. In no way was she how she depicted herself on the Net.

So the moral of the story is be careful, as always. Don't impart too much information about yourself and your family and if you do decide to meet, please let someone else know where you are going to be. Let them hover in the distance if needs be – better to be safe than sorry.

The health and fitness club

Probably one of my favourites; one of my friends started a business called Sporting Partners where you can find someone in your area to play whatever sport you want. Not only are you going to get fit, but you might well find yourself someone fit to date as well as a new circle of friends.

Also, if you are still seething about your break-up, ploughing up and down the swimming pool or pumping iron will do you the power of good, reducing your stress levels and getting you fit and looking great. Not only are the classes, gym and swimming pool great places to meet people but they usually have a social programme that you can join in with.

So although the first couple of forays into the bar on your own may bring you out in a cold sweat, soon you'll be on nodding and chatting terms with the rest of the club members, and many have probably joined for exactly the same reasons as you have.

Long distance relationships

Can be fun, if at times frustrating. Wonderful if you want to be committed but not under your lover's feet and fabulous if long weekends are your style of dating. Try to find your long-distance lover from a stimulating and funky city like London, Paris or New York! Or somewhere gorgeous and relaxing like the Cotswolds or the Lake District.

Be warned: LDRs are expensive. You must factor in all sorts of costs, like train or even air fares, petrol and mobile phone call costs. The main emphasis in LDRs is communication, because at times that's all you will have. You also need trunks, suitcases and bags full of trust to make it work.

Long distance relationships are only for those who find it easy to trust, have imaginations that they can keep in check, who like lots of space, lead busy lives and have a disposable income and can get away for weekends without too much notice or bother.

If you can handle it – go for it.

Mrs Robinson relationships – older woman/younger man

These are becoming more popular and less eyebrow-raising than ever before, especially the older woman/younger man combination. Some of our clients have opted for a younger man and their partners tell us that it's her sophistication and ease of handling herself and the world she moves in that's a big part of the pulling power.

Some chaps just prefer a lady to a ladette, probably because she has a pert brain and sharp line in conversation and opinions, as opposed to a pert ass and the capacity to drain a crate of alcopops.

Who knows? And who cares? As long as it's working for you, go for it.

It might be worth remembering that such a relationship may not stand the test of time. You may never plan your Ruby Wedding Anniversary party – at least not with your youthful lover – but it will bring roses to your cheeks while it lasts and at least you'll have lots in common with his mother!

The etiquette of dating

Be kind – everyone you meet is fighting a hard battle.

JOHN WATSON

Now, at the risk of sounding a tad old fashioned here, I do think it's worth reviewing how a date is supposed to pan out. So a look at good old-fashioned manners and putting everyone at their ease (because essentially that's what etiquette is all about) won't go amiss. Also, it could be useful as it may have been quite a while since your last date, especially if your marriage or relationship was quite a lengthy one.

Using Debrett's as *the* arbiters of social style, which they undoubtedly are on all matters of manners and polite behaviour, imagine if you will, that you and your dream date are just about to make that all-important rendezvous.

The chances are, even in these feminist days, that the man has done the asking out for the date. So please, blokes, don't turn up at the pre-arranged meeting place and bleat, 'What would you like to do?' You're the host – you should have worked that out; we are your guest – we are gracing you with our fragrant presence.

This is even more important to remember if you have asked a single mother out. We spend most of our days thinking about what meals to serve our brood and how to entertain them. The last thing we want to worry about is deciding where our date should take us – and here's a handy hint blokes, the average mother will eat virtually anything and anywhere providing she hasn't got to do the cooking or washing up.

Also, we don't know how much you can afford. Dinner at The Ritz would be nice but a good-hearted girl doesn't want to embarrass you if all you can afford is a couple of shandies and a bag of salted peanuts.

In fact, we don't even want you to spend a fortune on us. A walk in a picturesque area and a chilled bottle of wine al fresco is charming. A drive out to an olde worlde pub is perfectly pleasant too. Or a meal in a hip trendy brasserie that has just received good reviews in the local paper is cool. If you've put a bit of effort into the date and you make us laugh into the bargain you just might be on the winning straights. It's not that tricky, really it isn't.

If you are one of those men who does like to do something that little bit different (most girls dream about meeting such a man!), and you've planned a date with a difference please let her know without spoiling the surprise. If she turns up in kitten heels and you've booked an hour of tuition in a kayak the date might well not go quite as well as hoped. Likewise if she turns up dolled up to the nines and all you had in mind was a Burger King – this isn't going to bode well either.

The man must arrive on time but the lady is allowed to arrive just a little later. But be considerate – there's nothing more gut churning on a first date than to arrive and wait …and wait … and wait, feeling that the whole restaurant is sniggering behind your back.

If you are dining out and the menu is produced with a flourish – ladies, good manners dictates that you don't order the most expensive item on the menu or click your fingers and say, 'Hey, sommelier! Make sure the champers flows and let the good times roll!' Conversely, it could be construed as insulting to your date if you order the cheapest items on the menu, unless of course you find yourself out with Scrooge himself.

At all times throughout the date be charming and pleasant and that applies to both of you. Don't drown your dining companion in a rush of gratitude gush.

So let's assume it's all going swimmingly. Just a couple more first-date hurdles to clear and keep your fingers crossed you could be getting your diary out again to arrange that second date.

The arrival of the bill could be one of those sticky moments. Who pays? Well, if the man did do the asking out then by rights it should be him – no quibble. But there is absolutely no reason to stop the woman from saying, 'That was lovely but next time it's on me, agreed?' This seems only fair if you are earning much the same, and it allows the woman to have more control over how relations go from here.

Going Dutch is perfect if you never want to see the person again or if you are dating someone whose occupation doesn't yield as much as your own. Anyway, by halving the costs you can double up the outings – seems like a good idea to me. But on the first date get your wallets out boys. And if you find yourself dating a single mother do be considerate to the fact that she may have more expenses than you – paying for a baby sitter to name but one.

So you've wined, dined or supped and gawped at a cinema screen near you and it's a case of so far, so good. Just how is the best way to handle getting home? When my dad was courting his generation would think nothing of walking their date safely home even if it was a good few miles and in the rain, and all they got for their troubles was a peck on the cheek. Well, that's his story …! Nowadays it's rather different.

Far be it from me to lecture you on whether sex on the first date is a good idea or totally out of order. If the chemistry has been bubbling all evening then it may be difficult to call it a night, say *au revoir*, calmly hail a taxi and order it to the nearest cold shower. If you do want me to add my two pennyworth, I would advise against having sex on the first night. There's no rush and if you are both really keen on each other another couple of chaste dates isn't going to change anything in the grand scheme of things. Getting to know each other is all part of the fun, so why rush to the finishing post when you haven't even tested to see if you want to clear the water jump together?

So this is how the situation is best played if we are going to be quaintly old fashioned. Please drive the lady home if you are the one with the car, or vice versa if you are feeling kindly. Don't think for a moment that this means you will get invited in for coffee and extras. With an attitude like that you may blow your chances of a second date. If you have taken public transport, it is only polite to see that she gets her bus/train/taxi safely first. If a taxi is her preferred mode of transport then he can assume she will pay for it – however, if you *insist* on calling her a taxi then you should pay for it. But guys, let me tell you, you are in a win-win situation no matter what: if you call the taxi and you pay for it.

If it's all going horribly wrong

So your knight in shining armour has turned out to be more tarnished than the tin man with advanced rust and your dating damsel is taking on the characteristics of Kathy Bates' character in *Misery*. What to do?

End the date as soon as it is polite to do so. If you are dining out you can make your excuses and leave about an hour after you have finished the main course.

Be kind. Chances are your date has been crushed before so don't pulp their self-esteem any further if you can possibly help it.

Help preserve people's dignity by treating others as you would like to be treated yourself.

If the date really holds no hint of ever going further settle the bill by going Dutch. That way you can skip off beholden to no one.

At the end of the date, if you manage to stick it to the bitter end, thank your host and say as sincerely as you can muster that you had an interesting time. Peck them on the cheek or be really formal and shake their hand! And for good measure you could add a comment like, 'See you around sometime.'

Hopefully, they will take the hint that there is no mileage left in trying to get another date.

If you find that your date is turning into an absolute psychopath or an out and out bore, take yourself off to the lavatory, whip out your mobile phone and contact a friend to come and rescue you. If you fear being alone with them and no friend is on hand, have a quiet word with the waiting staff and ask them to call you a taxi. If all else fails climb out of the lavatory window. (A friend's mother actually did this – not because she thought her life was in real danger but because she was being bored to tears.)

Return to sender ... breaking up is hard to do

Well, not really. I mean it can be disappointing – they don't call this the crying game for nothing, you know. But if you've just had one or two dates then it's really no big deal. If you've decided it's just not going to happen then just let all contact slip. Don't return calls; don't text witty one liners that could be misunderstood; don't fire off chatty emails; but do politely turn down all future requests for your company.

However, if things have become slightly more involved then a rather more formal approach may have to be taken. Etiquette dictates that a clear break or closure is made so that the other party is quite certain that your relationship has come to an end and the reasons for this being so. Anything less and it's just plain cruel. The best approach is in person and in a neutral place – that is not the restaurant where you had your first date! If you really can't face a scene, and let's face it who can, a telephone call is the next best option. White lies are forgivable in these instances. Saying things like, 'You're so lovely but I don't feel I have the time/commitment levels/I'm not ready for a relationship yet' are all perfectly acceptable and you needn't go haring off to the nearest confessional box. Don't trade insults and try to score sarcasm points. Do keep your dignity – and theirs. Don't fill in the gaps. Women are classic acts for this. He's a bloke not a crossword puzzle. When a man says he doesn't want a relationship, guess what? HE DOESN'T WANT A RELATIONSHIP! That doesn't mean next month, next year or next anytime – it means now and with you.

And men, listen up. When she says she wants to be friends, she means just that. It's girl speak for, 'I felt more chemistry doing my GCSE retake in the lab when I was in the fifth form than I did on a date with you.'

Likewise, and this is for men and women, if your date is claiming they need more space than mission control then they don't want a relationship either ... and they don't fancy you.

Just move along. Don't grieve for what wasn't to be – you've already done that, remember. There are plenty more dates out there and with each one you are moving towards the right one and learning all the time.

6   *Relationships*

The first time you buy a house you see how pretty the paint is and buy it. The second time you look and see if the basement has termites. It's the same with men.

LUPE VELEZ

Y ou know that saying about not being able to please all the people, all of the time? Well with children it's questionable whether you can please any of them at any time, especially when it comes to introducing them to your new date.

The chances are your children won't take too kindly to you dating at all. Unless of course you manage to bag Prince William or Kylie Minogue and even then your offspring will beg you not to bring them into the playground when you're collecting them at going home time.

I dated a few men after my marriage broke up. But because deep down I knew they weren't right I didn't introduce them to my boys. Even so, I couldn't stop myself from racing ahead and wondering if this man could be the one to take on me and my sons, and love and protect us so that we could be one big happy family.

I made all the mistakes that any emotionally vulnerable person does, like getting involved with the wrong sort, having a relationship with a man who wasn't available because he was already in one. But even that didn't stop me from wistfully hoping that he would leave his partner to join me.

I cringe at these confessions, really I do, but I've found since running the Restore courses that many people make these classic errors. And it's a particularly common trait among us women with children. Many of us crave security and someone to look after us, whether that's fixing a leaky tap to putting their big strong arms around us when we've had a bad day. And there's nothing wrong or weak about that. Men tell of the same feelings – that they love knowing that there is someone out there concerned that they will get the 18.30pm train home safely and that their rugby kit has been loving laundered.

Then I used to torture myself with insecure thoughts like, if I did meet a man, who turned out to be the right one for me, then would he, could he, love my sons. I mean it wouldn't be his fault if he didn't; sometimes when I meet children I warm to some more than others. Or what if he liked them but they couldn't tolerate him? But then I got to thinking that life is full of ifs, buts and maybes and I made a decision that I wasn't going to let negative thinking get in the way of my future happiness.

I actually met the man who is now my second husband at work. The whole relationship began really slowly and was based on friendship to start with. A few work lunches here, a few after work drinks there. It wasn't until we had a 'proper' dinner date on a weekend night that I dared think this just might be the beginning of something. I was in therapy at the time, still suffering from the aftermath of divorce fallout, and my therapist recommended I have a 'fling' with him. In her experienced opinion it was high time I got back on the dating scene and I have to admit she was absolutely right.

However, for all I knew at that stage, my gorgeous new 'date' was going to return to his native South Africa. Anyway, I reasoned that provided I kept my feet on the ground, my head, in theory at least, could do a vertical take-off direct to Cloud 9 and all would be well.

It wasn't easy, I have to say. I was so nervous. My nerves were shot to pieces post divorce and my partner to this day jokes that back then I did a fantastic impression of a scaredy cat crossed with a rabbit in front of car headlamps. I was a dating disaster. Apparently I flinched every time he touched me. But I knew there was hope because the first time we went out to lunch he put my coat on for me and then fixed the collar rather like your mum does when she's checking you won't get cold on the way to school. I was so touched that he seemed so caring.

And so one date led to another and another, slowly, slowly, over the months. But more of how my relationship developed is covered in the next chapter. What I'm concerned with at the moment is yours.

Imagine you're going to hold a really important dinner party. You wouldn't randomly throw a few ingredients in the pot and hope for the best, would you? Surely you would spend some time choosing ingredients, dishes and wines that would complement each other and make copious lists to ensure you had everything you needed.

Well, choosing your next mate is a bit like preparing for that all-important event. Make a list of all the characteristics and personality traits that you would really like your next partner to have. And be careful you don't confuse character with personality when you meet that someone. What's the difference, you say? Here's an example. They could have you rolling in the aisle with laughter with their pithy and witty one liners – that's *personality*. But they might have dubious *character* traits, like being slow to put their hand in their pocket for their share of drinks or taxi fares or, more seriously, be chock-full of racial prejudice, which would really compromise how you view the world and all with whom you share it.

Do listen to your instincts. If it's heady passion you are hunting for their personality or character doesn't really need to be factored in, and if you feel sure you can handle the 'love 'em and leave 'em type' then fine. But if you're made of more delicate stuff then you really do need to let your head rule your heart. And let's be realistic here. It's doubtful that you are going to meet the perfect identikit man or woman on your list. But even so, by having a clear idea of what you do want you're less likely to end up with what you don't.

Another important aspect to writing a 'shopping list' for an ideal partner is to buck what that foxy lady Mother Nature *really* wants you to do. Now here's the science. All she's interested in is getting you to carry on the species. When you clock someone you fancy, your body releases a heady mix of oestrogen, testosterone, phenethylamine and pheromones. They cause your pupils to dilate, you to become tongue twisted when you try to speak to the object of your desires and your heart rate to go 'boom de de boom, boom, BOOM'. Those heady hormones make us more prone to go for potential breeding mates than for soul mates. Fabulous indeed for getting it on in the short term but not such a great love story combination for getting on with someone long term. So beat the old girl at her own game and just stay aware of what she's up to.

And I know I've mentioned it before but it's appropriate and very pertinent to mention it again here – before you break on to the dating and mating scene do make sure you are healed and fully recovered from post-divorce trauma. There is a danger that if you're not you will gravitate towards the type of character and personality mix of your ex-partner because you know the type and it all feels reassuringly familiar.

Needless to say if you do meet Mr or Ms 'Where-have-you-been-all-my-life?' only a few weeks or months after your recent split, mind how you go. Slow everything down and don't get carried away. You may have struck liquid gold or in your highly emotional state you may valiantly be pouring oil on troubled waters but shove the rose-tinted glasses to the back of the drawer.

How to handle those all-important introductions

The golden rule is to keep everything as low key as possible. No red carpets, no trumpet blast and cancel the sky writer – announcements on a grand scale simply aren't necessary.

Keep the early meetings casual and as brief as possible. And do cut the guilt; providing you are doing your level best to love and cherish your children then of course you have a right to a life outside the home and occasionally to live it in a bar, club or social gathering.

But you do owe it to your children to have someone trustworthy and fun looking after them when you are having valuable time off from parental duties and responsibilities.

Keep the introductions simple and no big build-ups or promises like, 'If you're good and nice to my new date, I'll take you to Legoland, Disney World Paris or the Moon.' Forget it. Just remember what your mother always told you – be yourself at all times. Children can see through a false show and if you're lucky they'll just rib you without mercy; if you're not they'll exploit your vulnerability and start adding a zero or two on their pocket money demands.

Do be prepared for the fact that your children may go a little strange on you. This is only natural, especially if they've been used to having you all to themselves. It really doesn't matter how old they are either, they just like to know that Mum or Dad is always there for them whether it's for pushing them on the park swing or collecting them from an all-night party. So be prepared for a few Kevin-ish tantrums.

Keep public displays of affection to a minimum with your new girl-friend or boyfriend. Most of us above the age of two years find them rather yucky anyway. So even when you're going through that 'I can hardly keep my hands off you' stage, no tussles on the sofa like lovesick Sumo wrestlers when the rest of the family are avidly watching East-Enders!

And if you do meet someone with whom you get on famously, the chemistry is there and you even have mutual hobbies but it all falls apart because they can't get to grips with the fact that you have children – no matter what their ages are – then worry not. Just bid them a fond farewell. It's not the new man's or woman's fault, it's not your fault and it's certainly not your children's fault.

When it's right, and you do meet 'the one' all the puzzle pieces will fall into position without too much movement on anyone's part – it's all just a matter of time.

Be careful what you wish for – in case it comes true!

So let's suppose you have met your man of the love match or the girl of your dreams, what steps can you take to safeguard your next relationship? Not surprisingly you might just find that one of the key points is communication.

We females are known to be good communicators, just think of those reams of emails we manage to send at work when the boss isn't looking or consider our monthly mobile phone and text bills. But when it comes to relationships we clam up faster than an oyster shell protecting a precious pearl. Fear and pride are often at the root of why we don't come out with what's troubling our minds and on the tip of our tongues.

Communication problems are cited as being one of the major culprits in relationship breakdown. And it's not because the couples in question are poor communicators in general – if they were then the problem would be understandable.

Research has shown that it is communicating with each other, which is the problem for most couples. Even those truly, deeply, madly in love birds find talking about certain subjects tricky; it isn't only couples who are avoiding speaking to each for some reason.

In my first marriage I was an inferential speaker – lots of women are – in that if my ex asked if I was fine, I would reply, 'Yes, why wouldn't I be?' But in fact my body language was saying the reverse (and the truth): pursed lips and folded arms spoke volumes. You almost had to have the gift of second sight to know what I was really feeling.

In the marriage I'm in today I no longer speak with a forked tongue but just come right out with what's bothering me. It's taken some time and it's an acquired skill but now I say exactly what I want or what I'm thinking.

For example, in the past and in my previous marriage if I wanted attention I would have slammed doors or sulked for England. Now, I say to my husband, 'I want your full attention so please will you face me, turn off the TV and listen to what I have to say.'

I don't do it because I've morphed into a ballsy bitch as a result of getting divorced but because I don't want communication problems to sour this relationship. And because he is a literal speaker – as most men are – he hears exactly what my point is and, being a man, that's the way he gains my attention. What a relief all round. I understand this now and therefore I don't get hurt by his direct speech patterns. This way we both know where we stand and there are very few communication problems. Result!

That's the way to do it!

At Restore we look at how you can communicate effectively and in order to do this you must become bold and brave, and say what you mean with love and respect.

So don't let fear of the consequences stop you from addressing issues.

When you are trying to confront someone, talk about the behaviour not the person, and take responsibility for your own emotions. No one can *make* you feel anything – *you* do the feeling.

A good example would be that a partner is working late – often a flashpoint for an argument: 'When you work late you make me really angry.' Swiftly followed by, 'I hate it when you don't come home on time. It can only mean you don't think much of me.' 'But I called to say I'd be late, you just don't trust me.' Can't you just feel the heat of that volcano of suppressed anger being stoked reading those words?

Through our programmes we look at helping people use a more constructive approach to the problem: 'I'm worried that when you work such long hours we don't get much time together, and I miss you. I'd like us to put some time aside each week that's just for us. Can we talk about that?' 'Yes, I see your point. Let's work something out then.' Phew! That's better.

Interestingly, though not surprisingly, many of our communication problems stem from the past. Adrienne Burgess in her book, *Will You Still Love Me Tomorrow?*, explains the importance of recognising triggers from the past that may impede the way we communicate with our current partners.

'Everyone has vulnerabilities,' Burgess writes. 'Emotional hot spots, which, just like physical weakness (proneness to headaches, back-ache or diarrhoea), can flare up when you are under stress. If being ignored by your lover reminds you of being ignored as a child, you may get angry when they are going through a busy patch.'

'Vulnerabilities,' Burgess further explains, 'are deeply embedded and unlikely to disappear. Indeed, how they are managed is an excellent predictor of lasting love. The future is bright when the couple can name them and work on modifying their own and accepting their partner's.' And as the Bible says, 'Speak timely words – be sensitive to speaking the right words at the right time' Proverbs 25:20.

No relationship is bombproof but how can you avoid calling in the disposal team?

You really want this new relationship to work, don't you? So let's count the ways and look at the skills that you can employ in order to stand the best chance of making that wish come true.

Support
Offer your partner lots of support – emotionally, physically, mentally and spiritually. Don't be backward in coming forward; tell them that you love them, back that up by helping them in practical ways: fix things in the house, cook delicious dinners, make their lives easier and more pleasurable in all ways. It's like the wise saying, 'Love is a verb, it's something you have to do, not something that just is.'

Compliments
Value your partner by complimenting them – when they look gorgeous tell them. Praise their quick thinking, abilities, good ideas, personality and intellect. And let them know you find them as scrumptiously sexy as your blood pressure will allow. It has a great pay off!

Honesty
Lies and mind-bending untruths are a relationship no-no. Be truthful at all times. It's a real confidence booster. And the more truthful you are at

the start of a relationship the better. It's so much easier to open up and show every facet of your character in a trustworthy relationship.

Expectations
Keep them realistic. Don't get carried away and don't hound your new partner into submission or force them into commitments they're not ready for. In all likelihood they've had just as nasty a scare on the relationship front as you have and don't forget that men tend not to bounce back as well or as quickly as we girls.

Listening
Learn how to listen *properly*; if you don't you're simply devaluing your partner as they speak. By paying close attention to what they are saying you are showing them that you care. Philosopher Paul Tillich went so far as to say that, 'The first duty of love is to listen.' And here's a sobering thought – if you really want your relationship to last – when you don't listen to your loved one, they will go and find someone who will.

Personal space
Give lots. It shows trust and, besides, it's healthy. Anyway, if you don't spend time away from someone how can you get that delicious feeling of missing them? And then you can look forward to doing something together that you have planned.

Diary of a relationship

It's not going to be the same for everyone of course but this account tells of one of Restore's partners, as we call our clients, getting over her divorce and going on a few dates before finally settling down once again.

> I've been divorced from my first husband for three and a half years. He left me and I have to say I've never known shock like it. It didn't exactly come like a bolt from the blue but nothing can prepare you for when it happens.
>
> I was Pete's secretary – that's how we met. He was a bit older than me, and a real charmer. I knew he was a bad risk; he was only 28 years old and already had one failed marriage –needless to say because he had an extramarital affair.

I'm afraid I fell big time for his seductive charms even though it was rumoured he was two-timing me with another girl in the company.

I accidentally got pregnant and we had a very hasty marriage. I thought I could change him and that the added responsibility of having a child would calm his skirt-chasing ways. Well, you can live in hope, can't you?

Now I know some people just aren't cut out for domestic bliss at all and I'm afraid Pete's that type. The nights out with the boys continued and stag weekends seemed to be permanently diaried in.

As an international salesman, Pete's work took him all over the world so the scope for having affairs was unlimited. It makes me shudder now to think how he took me in with his tales of bad mobile phone reception (I could never get in touch with him I wonder why!), and how he had to entertain business clients night after night. All lies. I eventually caught him out because he sent a text message to another woman but by mistake he sent it to my phone. I challenged him and he admitted it all. I think the pretence of the situation just got to him in the end. And he said being in a marriage was like being caged. He certainly was a beast to live with at times.

Even so, I couldn't help fancying him still, loving him a lot and he was such a good laugh at times. I missed him like hell; it was dreadfully painful; the emotional hurt was unbearable.

The day he moved his possessions out was the worst day of my life – it was so final – I felt like he'd died but he hadn't, he was still very much alive and living but no longer with me.

Every time my emotional wounds began to heal they would gape open again when he called to see our daughter – even a phone call would set me off down a spiral of deep depression.

However, as the months passed I begin to feel the benefits of counselling, which I desperately needed and my best friend made sure I got. Even I, in time, could see that I had been in a terribly destructive relationship which long term would have done me more harm than good. Being married to Pete meant never knowing true peace of mind. How can you live like that?

I stayed on my own for nearly two years until a friend introduced me to my current partner. I feel lucky that I met someone relatively easily without having to go through the traumas of dating. But to be quite honest I don't think I would have been strong enough to do that. When your confidence has been as hammered as mine has you feel you can't trust easily ever again.

Even now I can get paranoid when Dave's mobile phone goes and he knows I go through his text messages. He understands that trust is a major issue with me. We try to make a joke about it as much as possible.

The wonderful thing about Dave is he makes me feel so loved, in a way Pete never could or would. Pete was an alpha male – he had that certain something that women just can't resist. Pete's a playboy and Dave's a family man – that's the difference.

Dave's wonderful with my daughter and gives her the stability she needs – that quite frankly we both do. Pete might well bring her amazing presents from his trips abroad, but Dave gives her a regular presence. I know now which I prefer.

I went for looks and personality when I met Pete, but I was young, everyone can make a mistake. It's really no one's fault but it's taken lots of time to realise this. I'm no saint – I used to curse Pete every hour of the day for the hurt he caused. But now I've taken stock I realise that I knew what the score was right at the beginning; I just chose not to notice.

The key to getting over this kind of trauma is to take responsibility for your actions – it's really hard sometimes but we're only here once so why let one mistake blight the rest of your days? And never give up hope that you will, by the law of averages, find happiness again – that's the message I'd like to pass on.

What if your ex finds love again before you do?

This is going to be tough without a doubt. But let's analyse the situation.

When we think about someone who has fallen in love (like our ex), we get carried away. The contrast between our life – laden with new responsibilities, hassles over homework with the children, shopping, cooking, cleaning and stressful days at work – seems so harsh, we think glumly, as we picture the ex and their new love.

Funny how they are always strolling hand in hand on a beach, the sun never seems to set in their world and their way is always lit by a warm rosy glow. On the rare occasions they do leave the beach scene, they are dining *a deux*, having every need attended to by fawning and adoring waiters. Their nights are filled with passion and their days have a dreamlike quality. But stop the cameras rolling right there – it can't be like that because that's not real life and a living, breathing relationship is.

They have to go to work just like you do; their car breaks down; they have bills to pay so – surprise, surprise – sometimes there are overcast grey skies above that rose-filled garden of theirs. No one can stay in love in that hyped-up state forever. Not even you, I'm afraid, when your turn comes. Scientific studies have illustrated that if we're lucky that giddy infatuation stage only lasts for a mere 18 months. Then reality kicks in.

They may even be wondering if they did the right thing and with the right person. If they left you for the person they are now with it might be a case of leave in haste, repent at leisure. It takes at least two or three years to really get to know someone, so until you've faced a few traumas together how do you really know that when the heat's on you can survive the blast?

Even if they did do the leaving they will still have the effects of the grieving cycle to work through. If your ex founded their new relationship after you split up, but they haven't taken the time to make themselves whole, then they may be looking for their next partner to do the work for them. But no one can fill that empty void in another person created by lack of self-esteem and confidence. If they are lacking in these elements then the timing will be all wrong for a new relationship to stand a chance. There really are no short-cuts to recovery.

So don't punish yourself with what your ex is doing, might be doing, or would like to do and with whom. You don't know for sure, you're not in the relationship and don't let your imagination play cruel tricks on you.

Concentrate instead on gaining inner peace for your good and the good of all those around you. So keep up the good work – you're doing a grand job.

7 *Stepfamilies*

Children are a gift from God, they are a real blessing.

PSALM 127: 3

*U*ndoubtedly one of the hardest aspects about divorcing your partner is what to do about the children, from how to tell them your marriage and family life as they've known it is over to sharing their care.

'Getting them on your side' is highly tempting, and at a time like this touting for as much support for your team can become all-consuming. But please don't. If you have your children's interests truly at heart, you will know that in the long term this is stupid at best and totally inconsiderate and selfish at worst.

The world is a pretty scary place for children even when life is going well, but it could take on nightmarish proportions if Mummy keeps crying all the time and Daddy is so bad tempered he resembles something out of a monster storybook.

When the temptation to fall apart with the stress of it all arises, just try putting yourself in their shoes for a while – that might help put things into perspective.

I firmly believe, though, that the love of one parent is enough for children in a break-up situation. What I mean is, children will come through relatively unscathed if they receive continuity of care and know they are positively loved to bits. There really is little reason to fret that as a consequence of your divorce, they will grow up to be socially damaged, or be bottom of the class or turn into handbag snatchers as tabloid headlines are wont to convince us from time to time. Indeed, current research shows that divorce doesn't always have a damaging effect on children.

For every bullyboy son or daughter of a divorced single parent terrorizing the neighbours, there are dozens more children being raised by one parent or divorced parents who are quietly passing their Oxbridge exams, or learning how to apply a tourniquet at St John Ambulance first aid evening classes, or crossing old ladies safely over the street, or keeping their bedrooms tidy!

So in fairness to your children, just how can you effect a damage limitation project on what is possibly the most shattering event to happen to you and your family? You could try to follow these guidelines:

- Be really mindful of how they must be feeling. Children often feel to blame for the divorce. Irrational fears chase around in their heads – just like they do in ours – but they've got even better imaginations. They think the reasons for the divorce could include them not getting straight As in class or for handing their homework in late or pinching their baby brother when you weren't looking.
- Reassure them constantly and make it quite clear that you and your ex tried all you could but you just couldn't make the marriage work. And as far as humanly possible be upbeat about all the changes in your lives. Keep stressing the positive. Try to believe that it all will work out for the best and you will all be happier in the long term. Hang on in together and this experience will make you a strong, close and loving team. It's much more damaging and negative for children to have to live in an atmosphere of bickering and fighting and to witness a lack of affection between their parents.
- Don't use the children as bartering tools, especially in the law courts. It can be such a waste of money, time and emotional energy, all of which would be better invested in your children's welfare. As The Joseph Rowntree Foundation report (published 2003) warns, warring couples who resort to using the law to establish the arrangements for the children find that it, 'tends to fuel conflict rather than resolve it'. Try to thrash out as much as possible between you both and *never* in front of the children. Honestly, you will be glad you resolved as much as you possibly could when that final bill comes in from the solicitor.
- And don't use your children as emotional blackmail pawns in any ghastly revenge or vendetta against your ex, ex's in-laws, ex's new partner, etc. You know you don't want your children growing up damaged, in and out of therapy, unable to trust the opposite sex or experiencing difficulties forming lasting relationships, so don't drag them into the messy, mean aspects of divorce. It's not their fault they are

captives in this, so leave them out of the firing line. When the children are older they'll be able to work out for themselves just which parent was milking the situation with their own agenda in mind – and you won't get invited for Christmas and you'll die a lonely old man or woman – you have been warned.

- Do listen to what the children have to say and let them put their point forward. They are of a different generation and will have valid points that are pertinent to how society works today. It's no good harking back to what things were like in your day. Times have moved on and so should you.

- I know that sometimes you'll want to stay in bed, pull the covers over your head and stay there until the worst of Hurricane Divorce has passed by. So when you do feel like this just give your children a big cuddle and explain that today you are having an off day but everything will sort itself out in the fullness of time.

- Encourage your children to play or literally draw out their feelings. Energetic play, where they can act out their frustrations or use pent-up tension energy is good. My boys used to have regular bouts of wresting; consequently I've got quite a slick routine of headlocks, half nelsons and slam dunks up my sleeve. With drawings you can talk about the contents of the picture and get a good idea of what aspects of their life they are concerned about. But please don't tick a child off if they say something you don't want to hear; just stay calm and discuss the issue raised.

- Keep the children informed of developments as they happen or are about to happen and try to involve them as much as possible, like going to see a new house if you are having to move, etc.

- Try to find the funny sides of your situation – they are there. I once greeted my ex at the front door when it was his turn to have our sons for the weekend. I gave him their overnight bags and wished him a pleasant time and closed the door. A minute later he rang the doorbell. 'Haven't you forgotten something?' he enquired. I had of course – the children! Admittedly, hiding from the milkman because you've overspent the maintenance and can't pay this month's bill isn't so droll but lasting and valuable memories are made of the hard times, really they are.

- Don't use your children as go-betweens or messengers. If you need to communicate with your ex do it yourself – write a note, email or a letter. Barking orders and complaints at them like, 'Tell your mother

I'm not a bloody chauffeur,' or, worse, 'Tell his fancy woman to make sure she's got your school uniform ready on Sundays' is immature and unnecessary.

In a nutshell, you have got to be terribly grown up about the whole situation for the sake of your children. So don't be impulsive and goad your ex into reactions; there are no winners in divorce and do keep the children's best interests at the forefront of all decision making.

And there's no need to indulge children with guilt-induced presents. I'm not denying that divorce isn't a potentially traumatic time for them too, but this is one of the most valuable times in their young lives for develop positive attitudes about the blows that life hit us with. They will, if you angle this learning curve correctly, learn how to be diplomatic, to problem solve, to communicate well and to take on responsibility through adapting to these new dynamics of family life.

Children are a gift, they're fun and they help keep you poor! I mean they help keep you young, they're cool and they teach you new things about the world and they're most definitely worth keeping on the positive pathway to a new future – the one we are all on together, right?

When two become one ... and then some

The creation of a stepfamily is bound to be a bit daunting, especially when you look at it in isolation from all the other factors in your relationship, not least because there are so many people involved. There's you and your new partner, your respective children, the branches of your extended family, their branches of extended kith and kin and then each of your group of friends! But actually this very fact can be a huge positive after a divorce and as a result of forming a stepfamily.

There's a great part in Nick Hornby's book *About A Boy*, where the boy of the novel, Marcus, who lives with just his mother, realises that being part of a larger family isn't such a bad idea after all. 'Two wasn't enough, that was the trouble. He'd always thought that two was a good number, and that he'd hate to live in a family of three or four or five. But he could see the point of it now: if someone dropped off the edge, you weren't left on your own. How could you make a family grow if there was no one around to, you know, help it along? He was going to have to find a way ...'

When I compare how I was brought up to how my sons are raised, I realise that the close family unit I grew up in wasn't exactly ideal. My parents absolutely adored each other and never argued; they had an extreme, exclusive relationship and so rarely let anyone else in on their private world. Consequently, I grew up not having the skills to be able to deal with conflict – why would I? I'd never experienced it.

Also, there was a degree of social isolation operating in our household. There were no members of an extended family around us, no jolly teas around the table with aunties, uncles and a clutch of cousins. The usual teenage angst had to be suffered alone. Bearing all this in mind, I put masses of thought into preparing us all when we became a new family unit about six months after my new relationship started. It just felt like the right time to introduce my boys to my then boyfriend, Bram, now of course my husband and the boys' stepfather – don't ask me how I knew but I just knew.

Like our courtship, it was done with a very softly, softly approach. We dated in a serious way but nothing too heavy. I hadn't visited where he lived, nor he where I and the boys lived, until events took a dramatic turn. My divorce proceedings were grinding slowly through court. I admit I was still finding every aspect of it tough and disturbing. The trauma was obviously affecting me mentally and physically, one aspect of it compounding on another and as a result I collapsed at work.

Bram came to my office to ask me about a project we were working on and was told I'd been sent home. Like the proverbial knight on a white charger he thundered up the motorway as fast as his car and the law would allow him.

That incident pretty much cemented our status as a stepfamily. He moved in and looked after me post collapse and also immediately after that, when I had to have my wisdom teeth removed. You can imagine what I looked like post operation!

First he stayed in the spare bedroom so that the boys could get used to his presence and then, over a period of time culminating in a family holiday, we formalised our living arrangements.

My older son loved it when he came to stay because it made him son feel secure, because now there was a man in the house who could, 'fight off any burglars'. Kids – they think of everything don't they?

Bram's never made an issue of the fact that I came with two children and he has grown to love them as his own as the years have gone by.

Even an attack of nits and worms the children suffered from didn't have him haring back to his bachelor pad!

Even so, from time to time I had those relationship wobbly moments fuelled by insecurity because I was the one with the 'baggage', whereas he could up and leave at any time. I was obviously suffering from commitment desire – a typical female trait that I make no apologies for. He responded angrily to that, saying that he was as committed to the boys as if they were his own flesh and blood, and that he could no more walk out on them than I could.

During the third year of our courtship we were married by my husband's minister uncle in Cape Town, South Africa. I can honestly say it was one of the happiest days of my life. Tears streamed down our faces and my boys were there with all my new husband's relatives – our new family.

In addition to having a loving and secure bond with my husband and me, the boys maintain a close relationship with their birth father, so once again I see this as a positive aspect of divorce. Weekends away and shared holidays for our sons are beneficial for both them and all the adult carers in their lives as everyone has special time with them. My boys now have so many extra-extended members of their family. My new parents-in-law love the boys absolutely, and the boys have visited their family in South Africa and have a good grasp of the culture of that fascinating country.

They would never have had these wonderful experiences had it not been for my divorce. I firmly believe that a positive always comes out of a negative, and the best advice that I can pass on to you as one who has come through the worst of divorce is to concentrate on the here and now. Make your life and your children's lives as comfortable, stable and secure as you possibly can and don't let negative fears hold you back from making a new life.

As for those taking on the stepparent role, there are enormous benefits too. You may receive lots of love and companionship from your charges but you don't have to shoulder the major amounts of responsibility that the birth mother or father has to. You've been gifted with a ready-made family. You didn't have to go through sleepless nights; you didn't have to change a pile of nappies and you didn't have to go through the bizarre pregnancy cravings with your partner and get up in the night to make tuna baked potatoes with whipped cream and a swirl of raspberry jam. But you do get the kudos of teaching your new family how to ride a bike, swim their first 10 metres and play a mean hand of poker! New stepparents can have it all. Family life and days out at Alton Towers and you can still dip into your old single lifestyle like drinks with the boys or girls. But make sure you get the balance right between your new parental responsibilities and having some good old fashioned fun.

No one said it was ever going to be easy but after you've got over the introductions stage and survived a couple of trials by tea, stepfamily life isn't that far removed from 'traditional' family life. So take heart and a deep breath and come on in – the water's warm and the sharks have mostly had their teeth filed.

Top tips for all birth and stepparents

Agree to a set of house and behaviour rules with your new partner – and be really grown up about being consistent in applying them. Often there's a temptation for the stepparent to be lenient in order to get 'pally' with the children. Not a good idea, as children need and want boundaries. So even if you have to fly over Henry Kissinger to handle the negotiations, do call that rule-making meeting.

United we stand, divided we fall …and watch the children walk all over us. Children can be manipulative little beasts, so remember you're the ringmaster and hold firm when the ranks are threatening mutiny over discipline issues.

Do make sure you invest in quality time with your children without your partner. Make this time really special, so that your children know without a doubt that you value your time with them.

No one says it's going to be easy and of course arguments are going to occur between you and your new partner but please try to keep the drama to a minimum. Your children have lived through enough drama when you split up the first time around – so cool it.

Be patient. Depending on how old in years they are, how mature they are, or what level of understanding they can apply to situations, give the children time to adjust. You may have to accept that you will only ever be their parent's partner and never their new mum or dad.

Don't rise to the children's bait. If you sense they are being antago-nistic to gain your attention try to find out the root cause. They may be hurting over something and need you to listen, *really* listen, to the underlying problem.

Watch out for any regressive behaviour, especially in pre-school children, like wetting the bed or becoming excessive tearful or clingy. Children aged between six and nine years of age may have problems expressing their emotions and if they can't ask for reassurance their anxieties may exhibit as angry outbursts or difficulty in concentrating which may lead to learning problems. Older children in their early teens will be able to choose quite rationally which parent they would like to live with. Their choices should be listened to with respect.

Please don't hesitate to seek out professional help from a family counsellor if you feel the quality of an individual's or family life is suffering because of the divorce.

Don't let a situation escalate when, if dealt with appropriately, everything could be sorted out. It's all too easy to let a misunderstanding lead to the breakdown of a relationship or relationships.

Accept that we are all different. If there is another parent involved with sharing the care of your children take on board that they will have different methods of raising them. Only if you fear that abuse of a physical, mental or sexual nature might be taking place, or if such behaviour is threatened, then intervene and fast. If not, try to keep your own counsel and mind your own business.

Most children are loyal creatures by nature so don't make life awkward and embarrassing for them by criticising the parent they don't live with. They can recognise someone's shortcomings for themselves and they certainly don't need you to point them out.

Don't interrogate them after their visits to their other parent. Third degree inquisitions are not on. This is particularly important if your ex has a new partner and you're still cut up about it. If it hurts to know that they are planning a holiday to Bermuda and it's always been your dream destination or he's treated her to a Prada handbag, or the children were taken on a weekend extravaganza that you couldn't possibly afford, then don't ask for details. It's going to hurt like hell, so don't lead yourself like a lamb to the slaughter.

Give the children peace and privacy, and likewise they should give it to you. Everyone needs their space so build in a respect for this when organising the house rules with all new members of the family.

Take two stepchildren, add one birth mother, mix in a stepfather, fold in gently three children from the mother's previous marriage and decorate with a new baby ...

You might think that getting this particular recipe right would need the wisdom of King Solomon himself. I mean, imagine if your partner suddenly announced over an intimate lunch one day, 'You know, babes, I love you so much that I'm going to invite another partner to share our love, lifestyle and living accommodation. That okay with you? And could you pass me the horseradish while you choke on what I've just said?' Would you react with, 'Fabulous! I've always wanted a woman I can talk to after we've had sex and you've gone to sleep. Is she my size so we can swap clothes?'

Yeah right, I thought not. Resentful? Why yes! Upset? Highly likely. Murderous? Possibly. Put like that and we get an inkling of how our children might feel with the introduction of brand new or not so new siblings into their nest.

Let me stress again the importance of adjustment time, lots and lots of it, especially if you are contemplating remarriage. That means getting to know each other inside out, adapting to quirks and foibles in everyone's character – and we all have them because we are all highly individual. Boost every family member's self-esteem as often as possible. Happy, confident members of the family are a joy to bring up, the opposite pull everyone down with them.

And sometimes it's simply not going to be wonderful. Visions of packed bags by the front door and you running for the hills will swim before your very eyes; even the wholesome TV Waltons would have felt the pressure with a couple of stepchildren thrown into the family mix. But when the going gets tough be mature and act with kindness and dignity. Nine times out of ten all children want is encouragement, time and love and that costs you nothing. So forget buying lots of expensive toys – you can't buy their heartfelt co-operation, that only comes by giving them your sincere attention and being firm but fair when disputes occur.

Foster and encourage a real sense of belonging in every member of your family. As human beings we all need to know that we belong. That's why we join clubs, form communities and identify with certain groups.

Call regular family discussions where potential problems can be nipped in the bud. In a recent report on family life and eating habits published by the British Medical Journal, Professor John Ashton, director of public health for the North West of England, commented on the findings by saying, 'The family that eats together tends to stay together. Family meal times are a vital meeting point for parents and children to share problems, compare notes, discuss experiences and work at understanding each other.' So, repeat after me, 'eating around a family table helps to keep children stable' or go one better and have it made into a fridge magnet.

If you decided to make your union complete by having a baby together (and up to 50% of couples in second marriages/relationships do), do keep your expectations on hold.

Not everyone in the family is going to be thrilled. Some children will respond with a 'whoopee!' and others with a resounding, 'Yuuuk, oh pleeeeze,' and that's just at the thought that they know what you've been up to. Teenagers in particular would rather have third degree acne than acknowledge that their parents are having sex.

Allow for lots of communication to flow between you and all the children if they want to talk about the baby, and when the baby arrives let them help with caring for the infant, but again only if they *want* to. Don't force them. Babies, in the main, are rather cute and have a cunning way of getting most folk on their side sooner or later.

However, you must be as empathetic as you possibly can with existing children in the family so that they never feel they have lost their special connection with you. Imagine their hurt and confusion if they think that, just as their birth mummy or daddy was replaced, the same thing could easily happen to them? Constant reassurance is the key here and if you love them, tell them, and then tell them some more.

And take up the faith and become a believer in the resilience of children – with lashings of love and respect they will be fine.

How is it for them? Stepparents telling tales out of home

A *stepmum's* story

I knew right from the beginning that Jeff had kids from his previous marriage. I mean it's not a detail you can keep a secret and anyway, why would he? I think he told me on our first date. I was interested to know what ages they were but to be honest the fact he had children didn't affect my feelings for him as the relationship progressed.

The main reason for that is because they don't live with us, so I don't feel a huge and weighty responsibility for them. I leave the important aspects of child rearing and disciplining to the children's parents, that way they see me as more of a friend hopefully, which is the way I prefer it.

To date I haven't had any children of my own so my experience is very limited. On the rare occasions I have intervened on discipline matters, Jeff and I usually start arguing. He finds it amusing but I find it anything but.

For that reason my friends couldn't believe I had it in me to take on a divorced father of two. A few thought I was quite mad; think of all those Saturday nights you'll have to stay in when you could be out with us, they'd tease and my mother was very 'iffy' about the whole thing. But their reactions had no bearing on whether I would stay with Jeff; it's my life after all. I don't try to advise them how to live theirs.

Staying in and babysitting isn't such a problem because I've got a demanding job and I'm quite happy to relax at home at the weekends. But I do resent at times the attention Jeff gives his children, particularly if I've had a tough week and I want to talk it over with him, I feel I have to wait in line to get quality time with him.

And I sometimes feel left out on walks and outings because Jeff holds each child by the hand and they chatter away to him, which at times makes me feel like a spare part. I know it's immature but I'm only human.

Other aspects I would advise others to think carefully about are the financial implications of being a partner to someone who has children. They have always got to be provided for, through childhood, through school and college, to their wedding day and beyond.

Also, they've brought a child into the world with someone else, so you are aware that there was, and still is, a person who played a very central part in their life. I can get quite jealous of that too so I try not to dwell on the fact.

I am fond of the children but I don't feel an unconditional love for them. I'm not their mother – it's as simple as that.

Stepfather's family fact file

I must admit I did think carefully about getting involved with a woman with children. I mean you can't be irresponsible where children are concerned. When I told my family and friends about Angie and the kids, the usual response was, 'Why bother with the baggage mate?' That's such a narrow-minded opinion to take. So does that mean that anyone who's been married before or got children from a previous relationship should be written off? I don't think so.

As I'd always imagined myself at some point in my life with kids, either my own or someone else's it really didn't matter either way. Of course I didn't instantly love the children, those feelings take time on both sides to grow but I do now.

I think it's easier for stepdads, rather than stepmums, to take on the role of carer and to love their stepchildren unconditionally. And to be quite frank, although I get on with the Angie's ex, he's actually next to useless as a dad. Anyway, how do you define 'real'? Is it a biological function or a nurturing function?

The problems I run up against as a stepdad are exactly the same ones that I would if I were their real dad, like not going to bed on time, trying to skip their homework, being a bit lippy at times – so where's the difference? Kids are kids.

I'd recommend 'instant' family life to anyone but you must be sure it's what you want to do before it gets serious – you can't mess with kids' lives, it's just not fair – they've been through enough uncertainty during their parents' divorce.

And you're either the committed type or you're not. You want to make the role work or you don't – and I do. Everything about family life is easier now that Angie and I are married because we are a proper family unit. And I didn't have to go through early morning feeds and sleepless nights to get to this rewarding stage because the children were aged six and four of age when I took them on.

It's hard work, I'm not denying it – but it's fun.

8　Starting over

Marriage is a wonderful invention; but, then again, so is a bicycle repair kit.

BILLY CONNOLLY

I honestly think that anyone who says they don't want a warm, loving, fun, sharing, no-holds-barred passionate relationship, or that they haven't got time to have a relationship, is either deluding themselves big time, has been taking master classes in fibbing from Pinocchio himself or, more seriously, has been terribly hurt.

Everyone wants to know that in the eyes of their loved one they are the best thing to have walked into their lives since ... ever. No man is an island. I really believe that as a species we are not meant to be alone and no one can give you that 'I feel like I've won the lottery' feeling, other than someone you are having a happy, healthy, physical, mental and spiritual relationship with.

I also believe there are lots of candidates out there who can more than fit the shoes of 'the one'. You may have to kiss a lot of frogs before you find your prince or you may have to climb a lot of glass mountains before you rescue your princess, but they are out there, just waiting for someone like you to find them.

Finding your ideal partner is like enjoying the right mix of a Martini cocktail – it really can happen at any time, any place and anyhow. My friend's mother is still happily dating at 73 years of age – I joke not. And I know it might smack of 1950s advice to the housewife but once you are in a happy relationship, do watch your appearance – this applies to both sexes. Take pride in how you look. Don't cultivate a beer belly, don't pile on the weight or stop wearing make-up just because you are settled. Always strive to look fanciable and gorgeous. Attraction brought you together so maintain yourself; love enters through the eyes ...and leaves through the eyes. Don't get complacent; familiarity breeds contempt, remember. What price a slick of lipstick or a few press-ups to keep in shape?

If you've been paying attention, you will know by now that I bit the bullet and remarried, and very happily too. I wish I had the absolute blueprint answer to having a lasting and loving relationship, then I could explain it here in just a few succinct words and spread happiness throughout the kingdom like a fairy godmother. But I can't. And to be truthful I'm still finding out myself.

I think that having mutual respect is vital and feeling that frisson of physical chemistry is a must; meeting on the same spiritual plane is heaven sent and to be of a similar intellect is important too.

Of course we argue, bicker and fall out. We don't quite share the same sense of humour — what makes me cry with mirth leaves him blinking in bewilderment. British slapstick just doesn't float his boat. Likewise, what makes him laugh from the belly up doesn't so much as have my mouth twitching at the corners. But ...

So with my own experiences, and using those from people who have come on my Restore programmes, I've devised the following tips to help you and your significant partner to live happily ever after ...because, yes, I really do believe with due care and attention it is possible to do just that.

Ten top tips for future happiness

- Make sure you are fully reconciled with your previous relationship, what you did that may well have contributed to the relationship failure, and what you could have done that just might have made a difference. I can't emphasize enough that you do need to be 'restored' before you move on to your next long-term relationship. As this inspiring quotation explains, 'A new life begins for us every second. Let us go forward joyously to meet it. We must press on, whether we will or no, and we shall walk better with our eyes before us than with them ever cast behind.' (Jerome K Jerome)
- Now really be honest with yourself on this next point. Are you in a relationship because you really love them or because you can't bear being alone? Or is it because you feared you would never meet anyone again after your divorce, so anyone is better than no one? Are you wor-

ried that the older you get the less appealing you will become to the opposite sex? Were they the first dating candidate post divorce? If your answers are mainly yes then you must be realistic about where you want this relationship to go and if you want it to mature into something more. You should perhaps seriously address issues like low self-esteem because you don't have to 'put up with things' you know and as we are on Earth just this once why not try for the life you really want?

- Try not to agree to situations or discussions that you do not really agree with just to keep your new partner happy because you are afraid of losing them. In the long term you are not going to be able to carry on pretending that your are someone you're not. As the saying goes, 'your true self will out.'

- Keep the relationship alive and fresh; don't take each other for granted. Make sure you go out for intimate dinners, short breaks and days out on a regular basis to keep in touch with each other and to maintain that loving feeling. Just because you don't have the spare cash for romantic jollies – don't cop out. How expensive is a picnic blanket, a bottle of plonk and a few sausage rolls, and a drive out to the countryside? Come sun up, forget the chores and go and have some fun. This approach also has a great knock-on effect in keeping alive those delicious feelings of infatuation that most couples feel right at the beginning of their relationship. You can create and keep recreating romantic feelings, so make sure you do.

- Don't keep comparing your new partner to your previous relationship. Sometimes when something happens in your new relationship you become angry when you analyse the problem. When you've calmed down you will realise that you weren't being angry with your current partner. You were shouting at your ex-partner for all the pent-up hurt and anger from how they treated you, but you used your partner as the whipping boy. When a similar situation arises that caused a lot of friction in your previous relationship don't automatically assume that the same outcome will happen in this new relationship. Remember everyone is different.

- If your new partner has children, really work hard at not being jealous. It's not their fault they've been caught up as the passive players in their parents' divorce. I know it's tough, especially when they are rude, ungrateful, moody and playing each parent off to get the most favourable reaction. Often they are simply parroting what one parent has said about another. When they are adults they will be able to make rational decisions and evaluations about the differing roles of their parents and stepparents. At the end of the day you chose this life. You chose to take on a man or woman with children – *so deal with it.*

- Similarly, if your parents keep making favourable or flattering comments about your ex, or making comparisons, or even if they insist on calling your new partner by your ex's name, it's time to get assertive – and tell them to stop it. Your loyalty is to your new partner, you have made your choice and everyone must try to accept that. Make it quite clear that you appreciate their support to your former partner but your new partner is not to be made to feel second best. If your family have your future happiness at heart they will come to understand given time.

- Sometimes it's hard not to feel clingy or insecure with your second partnership, especially if you feel that you 'failed' for whatever reason the first time around. What if history repeats itself, you can't help taunting yourself. Don't be passive – learn from your mistakes. If you know you have a tendency to put your work first, make sure your schedule is more balanced so that you have quality time with your new partner. If you are aware that you have unrealistic ideas about spending, curb your habit – why repeat those money rows that soured everything first time around.

- Make sure you are mentally healthy because true happiness and contentment comes from within. Always work on your own self-confidence, self-esteem and, as I've said before, your self-image. You can't expect all this to come from your partner – it's unfair and unrealistic – take responsibility for yourself. We've all come a long way together but we really can't proceed much further on this journey unless we take these wise and true words by Louise Hay to heart, 'I forgive everyone, I forgive myself, I forgive all past experience. Forgiving everyone, forgiving myself. I am free. I am free.'

- Forgive and learn from your experiences and start to live again because with the right frame of mind, enthusiasm, commitment and attitude you can turn your life around … your divorce could be the best thing ever to have happened to you.

Each second there can be a new beginning. It is choice. It is your choice.

CLEARWATER

Mini guides

Selling your house and buying a new one

The eight main steps

As buying a home is both exciting and daunting we've included a brief guide that outlines some of the things you may need to consider to make the whole process stress free.

Step 1 – Decide to buy your own home

You've made the all-important decision and are ready to go out and find your dream home. Before acting on impulse, make sure you do your homework.

This is important because if you are used to living in a certain area with so many en suites you may need to readjust your standard of living to cater for the lack of income in your new household. It's a pride thing, though. Trust me, I moved from a five-bedroomed house to a three-bedroomed house and it was so easy to clean! And because it was small, nothing got lost, everything was put back in its place and I was not worried about people getting in somewhere without me knowing as it was a compact little house.

Step 2 – Find out how much you can borrow

The amount you can borrow will depend upon how much you earn and your other outgoings. Find out what your mortgage will mean in terms of monthly repayments and how much you'll have left over.

Try not to overstretch yourself in the early days, I wanted to move to a smaller house so that the kids and I could still be comfortable and that I could afford for us to go on holiday and if the worst happened and I lost my job I would still be able to afford the mortgage on a lower monthly salary.

Step 3 – Get help choosing the right mortgage

It really does pay to take time to consider the many different mortgage deals around these days. If you need advice on which deal suits you best and how to repay your mortgage, Bradford & Bingley advisers are well equipped to answer your questions. They have access to a wide range of other lenders' mortgages and can search on your behalf for the one that suits you best.

I ended up taking across my endowment mortgage from my previous marriage because we had not sorted the right advice in the first place. This mortgage is still with me because otherwise I will have to pay £7000 worth of penalties so I cannot recommend enough seeking the right advice, but make sure its from the right people and not just your well meaning neighbour or friend!

Step 4 – Search the estate agencies

Scan estate agents' windows for all their current properties. It's worth calling and registering with them so they can mail you property descriptions.

Step 5 – Get a solicitor

You will need a solicitor to help you finalise the legal aspects of your house sale and purchase.

You may find that the solicitor that you are using for your divorce has a conveyancing department so you may get all the services under one roof.

Step 6 – Get your chosen home valued

You will need to get your future home valued before you buy it. A basic mortgage valuation is the minimum you need but there are limits to what this will cover. It pays to check the property carefully and think about a structural survey that gives more information.

Step 7 – Finalise the arrangements and complete the deal

Many of the final stages of home buying are in the hands of your solicitor. They should complete your purchase as quickly as possible and keep you up to date, leaving you free to make your moving arrangements.

Step 8 – Move in

The day's arrived and the keys are in your hands. The property is yours. But the benefits don't stop there. This is just the first day of your life as a homeowner and if you've got the right mortgage, you'll enjoy the benefits for a long time to come.

I stupidly decided to cut costs when I moved to my new home and thought all my lovely friends would help me move! How wrong could I have been. I chose to move on a bank holiday weekend when everyone was away so I ended up with three friends who helped me move from a five-bedroomed house to a three-bedroomed house! Believe me I wish (and so do my friends!) that I had paid for that removal firm.

Attending your first solicitor's meeting

Make sure, when you go to a meeting with a solicitor, that you have prepared questions, and also the following information:

- Your Marriage Certificate
- Any correspondence or assessment from the Child Support Agency
- Copies of any Court Orders made in respect of this marriage or any previous marriage – or in respect of your children
- A letter which clearly states:
    o Your full name, and those of your spouse and children
    o Dates of birth of yourself, your spouse and all your children
    o Details of any children who are not issue of the marriage
    o Your address and, if different, that of your spouse
    o Names and addresses of your children's schools
    o Dates of any previous marriage of yourself and/or your spouse and dates of Decrees Absolutes
    o If you have already separated, the date and circumstances of the separation.
- A summary of your financial position; details of your income and that of your spouse, including welfare benefits; details of the home and its approximate value, and the name, address and account number of your mortgage
- Any other capital assets and any debts and liabilities
- Any correspondence that you may have received from your spouse's solicitor

How to employ a nanny or childminder

Before you look to choose a nanny we recommend that you follow these steps to clarify exactly what type of help you need.

Preparing a contract of employment

You need to make sure that whomever you employ understands exactly what duties they are to perform whilst in your employment. The contract should include the following elements:

- Start date of employment
- How much notice they have if you or they decide to end the contract
- Salary details which includes tax and National Insurance
- Hours of work
- The main duties involved in the role
- Offences for which you could dismiss a nanny
- Number of days leave permitted
- Sick pay allowed

Advertising for a nanny

There are several ways in which you can find your ideal nanny: some nannies will advertise their services on notice boards at the local library, shops selling children's goods or places where any children's activities are held; you can advertise in your local paper or magazine; you may also have colleges in your area that are training nannies and that you can approach to find a newly trained nanny. There are also agencies that will find the nanny or home help for you; these are more expensive than advertising yourself but they will provide you with a selection of people who suit your requirements. Make sure you double check any references they give you and get the agency to tell you how long ago they made their checks.

Interview process

Before meeting with your prospective nanny or child carer it is advisable to speak to them all over the telephone first and ask a few questions and give her a brief about what you expect from an employee. This will help you select which people you want to see and save you a lot of time interviewing people.

Once you have short-listed your ideal candidates you can then set about interviewing the candidates, usually an hour is adequate for asking your questions, finding out about them and making a decision on how suitable they are. Prepare a list of questions and ask each applicant the same questions. If you notice any gaps in their CV, which do not explain why they were not working for any period of time, make sure you find out what they have been doing when they were not working. Sometimes it's a good idea to have someone else with you so that they can ask any questions that you miss out, make notes and generally give you an objective view on each of the candidates.

Obviously you need to make sure the children are present when you carry out the interviews to see how they react to the prospective nanny and visa versa.

It's also really important that at the interview you give the nanny a clear idea of what the job is to entail, so if you expect her to do the children's washing and ironing you need to tell her. She also needs to be given some time at the end of the interview to ask her questions as well.

Interview questions for selecting your nanny

Make sure you write the questions that you want to ask her down and that you use this to make notes against so that afterwards you can compare her answers with those of the other candidates and so make your final selection.

You need to plan the interview well in order to make the most out of the time you have with each of the nannies. Here are some ideas of the sorts of questions that you should be asking to make the best selection for your children:

1. What made you want to be a nanny?

2. What do you like most about being with children?
3. What age range of children have you worked with before?
4. What experience do you have of working with babies?
5. What qualifications do you have and can I see the original certificates?
6. What duties do you carry out in your current role?
7. What other duties have you carried out in previous roles?
8. Describe a typical day when looking after your current children?
9. How would you fill my children's day?
10. What food would you prepare for the children?
11. What activities would you take my children to?
12. How do you envisage disciplining my children?
13. Would you carry out light housework, ironing and shopping?
14. Can you drive and when did you pass your test?
15. Do you have a clean driving licence?
16. Do you have any First Aid experience?
17. What would you say are your strengths/best points?
18. What are your weak areas/bad points?
19. What hobbies do you have outside of work?
20. Do you smoke, and if so would you agree not to smoke when you are in my house and with my children?
21. How long do you envisage staying in your next role?
22. If I offered you the position would you be interested?
23. When would you be able to start work?
24. What holidays do you have planned?

References

You must make sure that you follow up references, even if you find the nanny through an agency. Make sure that you speak to the referees personally and ask a few probing questions to make sure that the referee is a genuine ex-employer and not her best friend!

You can ask questions about the nanny's qualifications and make sure that you see the originals and not photocopied versions, e.g.:

*   NNEB/CACHE – Council for Awards in Children's Care and Education

- BTEC – Business and Technical Education Council – Nursery Nursing Diploma
- NAMCW – National Association for Maternal and Child Welfare – Nursery Nursing Diploma
- NVQ – in Early Years and Care and Education

Appointing your nanny

Once you have carried out all the interviews and collated all your answers you will be in a position to select the right nanny for you and your children.

If you have more than one suitable candidate it may be that you want to hold a second interview to be able to make the final choice. At this interview you could ask for them to bring their certificates and letters of reference.

Once you have made your final selection, and before you appoint anyone, you must make sure that you follow up her references, not just by reading the letters that she may bring with her but also speaking to people that she has worked for in the past.

Make sure that you get proof of her identity through her driving licence or passport to ensure that she is who she says she is!

Remember if you take on a nanny you will be responsible for paying her salary, tax and National Insurance so make sure you take into account what these additional costs will be so that you fully understand the total financial outlay.

And if you are in any doubt about someone, then go with that feeling and keep looking until you do find a suitable candidate.

How to shop for clothes

What to wear for that interview

Job interview? Important meeting? Returning to work? Your success depends on the image you project, so it's vital that you are aware of the impression you create. If you look good, you'll feel confident – and success is all about confidence. Your personal presentation contributes strongly to your impact and influence in the workplace and gives you the edge when it matters.

- Cover those legs; goose pimples and veins are not attractive at the best of times but especially when you want that job.
- Don't wear too much make-up; tone it down.
- Wear your hair in the way in which you would normally wear it; don't decide today is the day to have a new cut or blow dry in case it makes you nervous about it falling down at any minute.
- Depending on the job you are going for, dress appropriately.
- Use colours that flatter your skin; try and avoid colours that drain your skin, make you look sallow or ill.
- Try not to dress as if you are going to a funeral or a party; stick to something that is smart but not overpowering.
- Keep jewellery simple and to a minimum; again, you don't want to put on everything you own or have them stare at the Pat Butcher earrings!

What to wear for your first date

Difficult choice – you want to look good; you don't want to look like a mum; you don't want to look as if you are going on an interview; you don't want to be too casual: so what do you do?

It depends on where you are going for your first date, so dress appropriately, find out from friends what the place is like and what people who go there tend to wear, there's nothing worse than being turned away because you have jeans on and they are not permitted! If you are going to dinner you want to wear something that you feel comfortable in and that does not fall off your shoulders while you are eating.

- Take a friend with you to go shopping – someone who dresses well and likes shopping!
- Don't wear anything too low, otherwise you might show more than you intend to on the first date.
- Make sure that what you wear fits; try sitting down in it and see if your midriff looks a bit too overpowering or if it is hidden nicely!
- Don't wear trousers or skirts that are bursting at the seams when you sit down.

- Make sure your shoes or boots and accessories match your outfit. If you cannot afford a new outfit then go for the cheaper alternative by brightening up your accessories.

Personally, I hate shopping. I spend three hours in the shops and end up with nothing more than bags full of 'stuff' for the kids, sore feet and a bad mood. Well at least I did until I discovered the free personal shopping at stores like Debenhams. You can go in for two hours (or forty minutes if you hate shopping as much as I do), explain where you are going, what type of 'date' it is, they sit down with you and then bring back everything that is likely to flatter you and your budget and all the stress is gone!

First impression tips for women

- Before entering a room, say to yourself, 'I look good, I feel good'; tell yourself positive thoughts.
- Sit well, allowing for personal space, so don't sit on their laps but don't sit on another table and look frigid.
- Avoid crossing your arms or legs; this is a defensive action.
- Smile – make sure you know the difference between smiling and grinning inanely. I had to practise it in a mirror because I constantly had a furrowed brow after my divorce.
- Avoid touching your face, pointing or handling objects, picking beer mats to pieces or generally fidgeting so that you look scared. If you appear scared, you will act scared and end up scaring them off.

Appearance tips for women

- Have your hair cut every 4-6 weeks.
- Make-up is essential to create a professional business image. (I have also found that if you go into the department stores early during the week, when no one is around, you can have your makeover at the counters without feeling like an idiot.)
- Update your look with a current fashion style – but don't go over the top; seek advice from the personal shoppers or from friends who look a million dollars.

- Use colour on your face to enhance your appearance – I never used to like wearing make-up but it does make a difference to the way that you feel and obviously it enhances your features.
- Accessories are a simple and cost effective way to change your image.

First impression tips for men

- Enter a room confidently – head up, shoulders back and smile.
- Do *not* shuffle; walk at the same pace from the door to a chair.
- Handshakes should be a firm grip, *not* a 'wet fish' or a 'bone crusher'.
- Do *not* chew gum. Behave as naturally as possible, ensuring eye contact.

Appearance tips for men

- Always feel comfortable with what you wear.
- Do not try out a new look to create a first impression.
- Keep accessories to a minimum and use colour effectively. If wearing red make sure it is the correct tone.
- Keep aftershave to a minimum – we don't want to asphyxiate in it!

Going back to work

Finding work after a divorce

If you left your job so that you could stay at home for a while to bring up the children, the chances are that you are worried about how to get back into the world of work, particularly after a divorce when you confidence is low. Returning to the workplace after a long absence does not have to be frustrating so here are some tips on what to do.

Update your skills

If it has been a while since you last worked, it is time to find out which skills are currently in demand in your industry. Talk with people in the business, recruitment companies, HR departments and friends to find out what is considered to be necessary these days. Then either teach yourself or, if you can afford it, go on a course to catch up on those skills. Many areas also provide self-help groups to help women back into the workplace for very reasonable fees. Do all this before you start job hunting so you can includes these skills on your CV.

Get in touch with former bosses and colleagues

By far the easiest way to get back to work is to return to a place where you previously worked (that's provided you were happy there and left on reasonable terms). If you were well thought of they might be able to offer you a position. If there is nothing available, thank them anyway and ask if they know of any other positions or useful contacts that they might have who can help you in your hunt for a job.

Tell people

Tell friends, family, former colleagues, anyone that you know of who has an interest in your welfare that you are looking for work and they can also keep an eye out for suitable work for you. You could even give them a couple of CVs each with an outline of what you are looking for so they can pass them on to people who also may know of someone who is looking to take on additional staff.

Temporary staff

Probably one of the easiest ways to get back into a working environment is to join a temporary agency and there are all sorts of agencies around who place different levels of candidates in many different fields. This is useful to those people who also need to consider childcare and taking breaks during the children's school holidays. This way you can work when they are at school but also be flexible in having time off when they are at home.

Rebuilding a career

Don't be disappointed if you have to start in a lesser role than you had previously been used to; you still have an awful lot to offer, just get the basic skills they require under your belt and your maturity and life experience will prove that you are capable of more. All you have to do is take the job and impress your boss to get back to where you left off.

Jobs online

There are also a lot of agencies online on the net and companies also put job applications online as well. This means that you can sit at home and apply for lots of jobs in a short space of time.

It's also an effective way of showing the employer that you are computer literate.

Online forms

Company websites are also a great place for finding out about positions they have available.

Don't be tempted to complete and submit online immediately; take some time and care over it; print forms out and make sure that they make sense and are grammatically correct.

The forms will ask for optional and compulsory information, so complete all the sections in order to give a more detailed account of you and your work experience so that employers are given an insight into who you are, what you are looking for and what you are capable of.

Remember to save copies of applications that you have filled in, along with the name and details of the company that you have applied for a position in.

Downloadable forms

Some companies may also offer a form that you can download onto your computer, fill in at your own speed and print off and read, making changes and then editing the document before sending it back to the employer, either by email or by post, whichever they have requested.

Email applications

Email can be seen as a very informal way of approaching people. However, if you are asked to send information to an email address, treat it formally. Make sure you send a covering letter and a CV as you would if you were applying by post.

CV tips

The aim of this short guide is to equip you with the necessary skills and knowledge with which to secure you the next step in your career progression.
We will look at the following:

- How to prepare the perfect CV for you.
- How to prepare for an interview.
- How to present yourself at an interview.
- How to respond to difficult interview questions.
- How to close the interview.

How to prepare the perfect CV fact sheet

What is a Curriculum Vitae?
1. It's the initial sales tool that you have in order to sell yourself, your experience, knowledge and skills to the company.
2. The CV must sell you and your skills above everyone else's to the potential employer.

3. You must remember that employers receive hundreds of applications for a job and you need to ensure that you don't get passed over.

What puts off a potential employer?
- The paper is poor quality.
- There are spelling mistakes.
- A cluttered CV.
- Too many pages of information.
- Personal information at the front instead of work-related experience.
- The CV is not relevant to the job advertised.

What would make a potential employer want to interview you?
- No spelling mistakes.
- A CV that is no more than two or three pages long.
- Work experience at the front and personal details at the back.
- Relevant experience highlighted.
- Experience of solving problems, generating money or saving time: all things employers are looking for a new employee to help them with.

Before you begin to write your CV look at the job advertised. Pick out the elements that you have experience in or can show that you have an aptitude for.

Now make a list of all the functions that your job entails that are relevant to that job. Using those functions create 'action' statements, which will describe not only what you do but also what you have achieved in doing that particular function.

When you send your CV off for the advert tailor your covering letter to include some of the skills and phrases that they have indicated they are looking for and incorporate them into your letter.

Don't have one CV for every job that you apply for or one covering letter, adapt each one for the job as each job and company are different and looking for different experience.

How to prepare for an interview

You need to prepare the following components to have a successful interview:

- Company Information
- Your preparation
- Transport
- Questions

What company information do you need to prepare?
- What business the company is in, is it a good marketplace, declining, successful?
- Look up their website, library, company marketing material, their customer services department, local newspapers, friends or colleagues to find out more about them.
- Find out if the company is profitable or not.
- Where they are located?
- How long have they been established?
- Is it a new venture?
- Who are their customers?
- Who are their competitors?

What do you need to prepare?
- Your clothes: do wear a suit or co-ordinating clothes; clothes need to be appropriate to the job you are applying for.
- Choose colours that do not drain you or make you look ill or tired!
- Don't try and be too fashionable, wear too much jewellery, make-up, perfume or after-shave or uncomfortable shoes.

What about your transport?
- Make sure your car has enough petrol in it!
- Make sure you leave enough time to get there promptly.
- Make sure you know the directions.
- It's better to get there early and wait in reception than arrive late

What questions should you ask?
- Always prepare a list of sensible questions to ask when you are at the interview; there is nothing more off-putting than someone who applies for a job but then does not want to ask anything about the company.
- Don't make your first question 'How much holiday will I get?' or 'When do I get a pay rise?' or 'When can I get promoted?'
- Do make your first questions something like these:

- What initial training programme is offered with this position?
- Having proved myself in this role over an 18 month to 2-year period, what career progression would be available?
- What courses outside of work could I do to assist in my role?
- How long has this department been going?
- What is a typical day in this department likely to be?
- How do you compare with your nearest competitors?

How to present yourself at an interview

- Walk in and offer a FIRM handshake; always offer your hand first.
- Make sure your notes and bags are in your left hand so that your right hand is free to offer.
- Make sure your body language is positive throughout the interview.
- Try not to twist or cross your legs too much.
- Make sure your hands are on the arms of the chair, not crossed in front of you or under your bum!
- Sit up straight and make sure that when you answer questions you look the interviewer in the eyes.
- If there is more than one person conducting the interview include them all as you answer by looking at each one in the eyes as you answer.
- Smile occasionally but don't grin inanely!
- Whatever you do, don't:
  - only look at one person,
  - cross your arms,
  - sit on your hands,
  - cover your mouth with your hand,
  - close your eyes whilst you answering a question,
  - sniff,
  - shuffle in your seat.

How to respond to difficult interview questions

- **What do you dislike about your present company?**
  That's a hard question as I enjoy the job I do currently and the opportunities I have been given by the company. My wishing to leave

is to further enhance my skills, experience and knowledge and not because I dislike the company.

- **What would you say is your biggest weakness?**
  In the past my writing skills used to let me down so, having recognised that as a development area, I completed a writing skills course.
  (Pick on an old weakness that happened in the past and show how you overcame it.
  If pushed by the interviewer, then answer that any weak areas fed back to you by your manager have always been welcomed and you have worked towards developing them.)

- **What is your current salary?**
  With my current role the salary is commensurate with the tasks and responsibilities. This role is clearly looking for someone to '..., ...' so is not a direct comparison. What salary is on offer?

- **What is the most difficult issue you have dealt with?**
  One of the most difficult tasks was ..., it was difficult because of ....
  I succeeded in rectifying this situation by creating an action plan of how to move forward.

- **Name five of your strengths?**
  (Remember – the advert tells you what they are looking for so prepare some statements of strengths, incorporating what they are looking for into your examples.)

- **Why should we give you this job?**
  I believe my experience in ... and my knowledge of ... clearly demonstrates my ability to succeed and provide solutions for a company like you.

How to close the interview

Always say at the end of the interview:
Having met me and read my CV do you have any reservations about recommending me for this position?

Or

> I feel that I have all the necessary skills and experience to be able to make a valuable contribution to your company and would relish the opportunity to show you. Will you be giving me that opportunity?

Or

> After this interview today will you be in a position to offer me this role?

I have interviewed plenty of people in my working career and it never fails to amaze me that people will leave an interview and worry about whether or not they are going to be called back. Remember, you are also interviewing them to see if you like them and want to work there, so employers will expect you to show that you want to work there and one way of doing this is asking 'will you be offering me this job?' You don't have to be fancy about asking the question but be direct.

It must be far easier to go home at least knowing that they have several other people to see before they can make a decision or that they are concerned that you don't have enough experience in a certain area. At least you know and you can start working out how to counter that, so explain that if there is a weak area you are more than happy to go for any additional training that they might suggest which will help.

Make life easier for yourself by asking what their intentions are.

How to handle your ex ... and their new partner

- Try to limit the amount of 'day dreaming' you have about situations, or arguments that you could have with them. This will wind you up and make you feel very negative.
- When they call or visit and say something that upsets, frustrates or makes you angry, DON'T react. You can't control how they behave or what they say to you but you CAN control how you react! When you become angry they have achieved what they wanted to, they go away satisfied that you are now angrier, more upset and therefore they still have some influence and control over you and your life. By NOT re-

acting they do not have that influence or control: YOU do, and that is what you want to achieve!

- Do not, however difficult it is, be tempted to make derogatory comments about your ex to your children. They love your ex, no matter what he/she has done to you, and you have to remember that you are the adult in this situation. In the long term, you will be glad that you did not make your children take sides, they will grow up healthier and happier.

- Do not ask your children what they did when they were with the ex, do not pump them for information about the ex's lifestyle, partners, financial situation. This is unfair on the child and will have lasting effects upon them.

- If your ex insists on sending you long emails, letters and voicemails do not react. Ignore them! If they persist, then report them to the police but do not become embroiled in lengthy discussions through these mediums as you are again allowing them to control you and your life.

- Make sure that any agreement that you have with your ex over assets, financial investments and access to the children takes the form of a written agreement. Many times the ex-partner will promise that you will be looked after, yet, when a new person enters their lives this promise is not always honoured. Although they may mean what they say now, will they mean it in the future? It's better to be safe than sorry, so get it documented.

- Allow yourself to grieve over the loss of the relationship but do not wallow in self-pity. You have an enormous amount of time in your life left – do you want to spend the next 30 years wallowing in misery or do you want to enjoy life to the full?

- At some point in your grieving cycle you will accept that the relationship is over, you will be able to forgive both yourself and your ex-partner for the relationship mistakes that you both made and you will learn from those mistakes. Remember, a mistake is only a mistake if you don't learn from it. If you learn from a mistake it's called an 'experience'. So forgive yourself and move on with your life!

- Revenge! Better to think it than actually do it! If you are consumed by thoughts of revenge, think very carefully about what the consequences of that revenge will be, who else it will affect, and how it is likely to affect them. If you are feeling vengeful, write it down and read it, but don't be tempted to become vindictive, however tempting it is at the time! By having such feelings of hate, you are still in a relationship with your ex and why waste energy on them when you could be spending that energy on yourself!

- Do keep a record of the facts – things that actually happened – because as time passes, with each person you talk to about your ex-partner stories become more elaborate, until your ex-partner resembles the devil! You need to keep some perspective on what actually happened, so keep the documentation you gave the solicitor on the real and truthful reasons behind the divorce. This enables you to retain perspective later on and will help if your children, when much older, want to know your version of the truth. And remember, we all see things from different angles: just as you believe your version, your ex will be adamant that their version is the truth as well. Life does not seem to get any easier until you accept that there are always several versions of the event!

Summing up

*D*ivorce – confrontations with a confusing legal system, big bills, lonesome single life, disastrous dating, fretted myself into losing weight, blissed out and blossomed and put it all back on again, formed a new relationship and took that leap of blind faith and courage back into my second marriage.

So was it all worth it? That's a question I'm asked time and again, usually by those taking their first tentative step towards ending their wedded union. And I have to say, hand on my heart, Yes! Yes! Yes! It was, it is. I feel like punching the air when I answer but I think they get the message loud and clear.

Life to me is so much brighter now. I appreciate every aspect of my existence, I realise I've been given a second chance and I'm not going to waste it.

Making a new life can be, and is, painful – there is no getting away from it. Just the recovery time alone needs to be toughed out and then there is the spectre of the rest of your life to work on. I honestly thought I would be completely sorted out emotionally, physically and spiritually in just six months from the time I decided my marriage had come to the end of the line. How naïve of me, I realise now.

And just when you think you've grasped and clawed your way to the top of one seemingly insurmountable problem and you're enjoying the view, made all the more glorious for your efforts, sure enough a reminder from the past will send you reeling off your emotional plateau.

It actually took me about 18 months to recover from my seven-year marriage. And that was just the sharp shock pain. To my amazement I was still feeling the dull depressing effects of emotional fallout for even longer than that. Even today, I'm still not totally immune, I find that totally unrelated arguments, like one I had with one of my in-laws or a dispute I had with my brother, can send me back into a downward spiral of despondency or a craving for a cigarette – a vice I got into at the zenith of my troubled divorce times and have not touched since. Sometimes it can be hearing a favourable comment about my ex's partner – the same feelings of anger, hurt, frustration, and that awful shaky sick sensation in my stomach can come back, and realistically they may always do. However, they are not as strong and they grow weaker each time they reappear.

If this happens to you too, don't get too despondent or feel that you aren't making any progress at all – *you are*. You're making constant headway, even feeling like I've just described is progress, because what you will find is that you don't feel like this for very long. Since you made that important break or had it made for you, you have been developing coping mechanisms and these kick into action every time you need their assistance. You will bounce back much, much quicker after another nasty shock or a particularly bloodcurdling argument and then you will discover that bouncing back turns into a mere shrug of the shoulders and even a wry chuckle. That's true recovery and more often than not it will happen if you really try.

You're learning all the time to deal with situations. Indeed, we never stop refining and defining ourselves and finding our own style of coping is a fantastic achievement to be well and truly proud of.

And along the way I really think I've become a nicer person, probably because of all the soul searching and tough times I've been through. I'm certainly no longer guilty of being as judgemental as I might have been before and that makes me notice when others sit in judgement of others. The worst usually comes from people who shy away from those they see as having 'baggage'. But we all have baggage when you think about it. Some of us started carrying it because of childhood experiences, others perhaps picked some up when their parents got divorced. Others have right up to the minute stuff if their relationship has suddenly gone belly up.

And anyway, who am I to judge others? Just as 'they' have no right to judge me. We all make our choices in life and sometimes they work and sometimes, for the lack of information or haste or whatever reason, those choices simply don't work. *C'est la vie*. It could happen to any one of us and more than likely has if statistics are right.

Life, I think, is a never-ending circle, or a Merry Go Round if you like, that we hop on and off. You may think that your turn has come to an end and you'll never know happiness and pleasure again – but honestly it hasn't.

It's waiting for you to join all the other assembled passengers; it's just down to you to choose when you're ready. And if you need a bit of help, just call us at Restore for a word of advice or news of our latest courses.

Restore provides practical advice and guidance to help people who are going through a life crisis such as divorce, bereavement, redundancy or retirement. We provide evening events that help you unravel legal, financial and emotional issues that you have, and help put you on the right path for building a brighter future.

For more information about Restore, visit their website: www.restoreprogramme.com

Contacts

- FMA: Family Mediators Association. Contact 0117 946 7062 (PO Box 5, Bristol BS99 3WZ).
- NFM: National Family Mediation. Contact 0207 485 8809 (Star House, 104-108 Grafton Road, London NW5 4BD). www.nfm.u-net.com.
- ADR Family: ADR Group Family. Contact 0117 946 7180 (ADR Group, Family Mediation Training, Grove House, Grove Road, Redland, Bristol BS6 6UN). www.adrgroup.co.uk or email: info@adrgroup.co.uk.
- SFLA: Solicitors Family Law Association. Contact 01689 850227 (PO Box 302, Orpington BR6 8QX). www.sfla.co.uk
- UKCFM: UK College of Family Mediators. Contact 0117 904 7223 (Alexander House, Telephone Avenue, Bristol BS1 4BS). www.ukcfm.co.uk or email ukcfm@btclick.com

Recommended reading

Shortcuts to bouncing back from heartbreak by Gael Lindenfield (HarperCollins, 2002)

Debrett's New Guide to Etiquette & Modern Manners by John Morgan (Headline, 1999)

Will You Still Love Me Tomorrow? by Adrienne Burgess (Vermilion, 2002)

Hot Relationships by Tracy Cox (Corgi Adult, 2000)